Differentiated Instruction:

A Guide for Foreign Language Teachers

Deborah Blaz

EYE ON EDUCATION
6 DEPOT WAY WEST, SUITE 106
LARCHMONT, NY 10538
(914) 833–0551
(914) 833–0761 fax
www.eyeoneducation.com

Library of Congress Cataloging-in-Publication Data

Blaz, Deborah.
Differentiated instruction : a guide for foreign language teachers /
Deborah Blaz.— 1st ed.
     p. cm.
  Includes bibliographical references.
  ISBN 1-59667-020-7
1. Individualized instruction. 2. Languages, Modern—Study and teaching.
I. Title.
LB1031.B63 2006
418′.0071—dc22

                                                                2005035
388

10 9 8 7 6 5 4 3 2

Editorial and production services provided by
Richard H. Adin Freelance Editorial Services
52 Oakwood Blvd., Poughkeepsie, NY 12603-4112
(845-471-3566)

Also Available from EYE ON EDUCATION

**Bringing the Standards
for Foreign Language Learning to Life**
Deborah Blaz

**A Collection of Performance Tasks and Rubrics:
Foreign Languages**
Deborah Blaz

**Foreign Language Teacher's
Guide to Active Learning**
Deborah Blaz

Teaching Foreign Languages in the Block
Deborah Blaz

**Handbook on Differentiated Instruction
for Middle and High Schools**
Sheryn Spencer Northey

**Differentiated Instruction:
A Guide for Middle and High School Teachers**
Amy Benjamin

**Differentiated Instruction:
A Guide for Elementary School Teachers**
Amy Benjamin

**What Great Teachers Do Differently:
14 Things That Matter Most**
Todd Whitaker

**Seven Simple Secrets:
What the Best Teachers Know and Do!**
Annette Breaux and Todd Whitaker

**Classroom Motivation from A to Z:
How to Engage Your Students in Learning**
Barbara R. Blackburn

About the Author

Deborah Blaz, a French teacher at Angola High School in Angola, Indiana, is a native of St. Charles, Illinois. She received her BA in French and German from Illinois State University, a *diplôme* from the Université de Grenoble in Grenoble, France, and, in 1974, an MA in French from the University of Kentucky. Ms. Blaz has taught French and English to grades 7 through 12 for the past 26 years in Indiana. She also serves as foreign-language department chair at her school and does professional translation work.

Ms. Blaz is the author of four best-selling reference books: *Foreign Language Teacher's Guide to Active Learning; Teaching Foreign Languages in the Block; A Collection of Performance Tasks and Rubrics: Foreign Languages;* and *Bringing the Standards for Foreign Language Learning to Life.* She has frequently presented on successful teaching strategies at state, regional, and national conferences, universities, and high schools. In 1996, she was named Indiana's French Teacher of the Year by the Indiana chapter of the American Association of Teachers of French (IAATF) and was named, by *USA Today,* to the All-USA Teacher Team, Honorable Mention. She was a recipient of the Project E Excellence in Education award in 2000.

She may be contacted at Angola High School, 350 South John McBride Avenue, Angola, Indiana 46703, or by e-mail: dblaz@msdsc.org.

TABLE OF CONTENTS

1

Differentiated Instruction: From Content to Process to Product

If someone were to ask you what's new in education, what would you say? I know what my answers would be:

- Increased emphasis on testing and standards

- Brain-based teaching strategies

- The emphasis on and explosion of variety in learning styles and how to appeal to them

- The paradigm shift in curriculum from what topics should be taught to what students will be able to demonstrate (emphasis on performance)

- Technological emphasis and advances

- Movement away from tracking and toward mixed-ability classrooms, including mainstreamed students with Individual Student Profiles, as well as students with attention deficit/hyperactivity disorder or attention deficit disorder (ADHD/ADD)

- Differentiated instruction and its effectiveness in any classroom

What Is Differentiated Instruction?

This term encompasses a wide range of teaching strategies and attitudes that focus on the two concerns of any good educator: students and learning. The standards and curriculum tell us what students need to know, and differentiated-instruction techniques help us get them there while we teach them how to learn.

Is It Something New?

No. It has been around for at least two decades, for gifted and talented students (those working above grade level). About 8 or 10 years ago, teachers began using it for special-education students as well (those working below grade level). So, what's new is the notion that it can work for *all* students.

Differentiated instruction is somewhat hard to define. Let's start with the definition provided by permission: from *Merriam-Webster's Collegiate® Dictionary, 11th Edition* and *Merriam-Webster's Collegiate® Thesaurus* ©2005 by Merriam-Webster Inc. (www.Meriam-WebsterCollegiate.com):

> *Differentiate:*
>
> transitive senses:
>
> 1. to mark or show a difference
> 2. to develop differential characteristics
> 3. to cause differentiation of in the course of development
>
> intransitive senses:
>
> 1. to recognize or give expression to a difference
> 2. to become distinct or different in character
> 3. to undergo differentiation
>
> **Related Words:** comprehend, understand
>
> **Contrasted Words:** confound, mistake
>
> **Antonyms:** confuse

In differentiated instruction, the teacher must be the transitive, and the student is intransitive!

As the definition above indicates, (1) Teachers must mark or identify the differences both in students and in possible teaching strategies, and make adjustments according to what will most benefit students and best facilitate learning in the classroom. (2) Teachers will then develop and implement, bit by bit, the characteristics of a differentiated classroom. (3) The key word is *development*. Any good educational program is always under construction: Assessment, evaluation, and reflection are the keys to finding what works and what doesn't work, and the key to trying to fix the latter.

Continuing the definition, with students as the intransitive aspect, students must learn to recognize their differences, their strengths and weaknesses, their learning styles and intelligences, and how to deal with those and find the best way to express them. They must develop the confidence and self-esteem so necessary for learning.

What Differentiated Instruction Is

- ◆ Complex and flexible, with many ways to accommodate different teaching styles as well as student differences in the following:
  - Learning styles
  - Interests
  - Prior knowledge
  - Socialization needs
  - Comfort zones
- ◆ Rigorous: providing challenging instruction that motivates students
- ◆ Relevant: not more of the same, and not fluff, but essential learning
- ◆ Proactive: using methods like hands-on projects

The best differentiated classrooms are based on certain beliefs and practices. Here is a list of those (organized alphabetically rather than by importance, as the items are equally important):

- ◆ *Choice.* Students in a differentiated classroom have a choice in what they learn, how they learn it, and how they show the knowledge they have. They are less likely to learn well if the teacher makes all the decisions. "The best learning environment offers a large variety of choices to satisfy individual abilities and talents" (Jensen, 1998, p. 30).

- ◆ *Connections.* New learning gets stored in the long-term memory when a connection is made between it and a student's previous experience, knowledge, or interests. This is why one of the five C's in the national standards is connections: connections to students' language, to other students and the teacher, to things learned in other classes, or to the community and the world. Any connectedness has a positive effect on learning and is a major goal of any differentiated-instruction lesson.

- ◆ *Learning how to learn.* The teacher should take time to make the students aware of how they learn best and to teach them strategies that will benefit them inside and outside the classroom.

- ◆ *Multiple learning modes.* Brain research tells us that there are many different learning methods, including inquiry, memorization, technology, and socialization. In a differentiated classroom, both the students and the teacher learn new learning methods.

Teaching is an art, and every teacher is different. We all know the value of humor and enthusiasm, communication and intuition, as well as a love of our subject matter and our students, whether we teach using a text or Total Physical Response Storytelling (TPRS). Differentiating does not mean you need to change what works for you; it asks that you consider expanding your repertoire to see if you can reach a few more students. The more techniques you can use, the better the students will learn.

- ◆ *Open-endedness.* Assume that learning never ends and that thinking about a topic should continue. Sometimes thinking generates more questions (curiosity is a great stimulant of knowledge), instead of just a single answer. Strategies like Socratic seminars and many upper-level Bloom's activities (see Chapter 4) are open-ended.

- ◆ *Routine.* In addition to making students feel secure and establishing expectations for the classroom—and therefore establishing teacher control of that environment—routine can trigger memories of facts learned. Structure is important.

- ◆ *Student talk.* There should definitely be times when the teacher is talking and students listen or take notes or copy off the board, but any classroom should be communicative and interactive in nature.

- ◆ *Variety in instruction and assessment.* Variety can bring excitement and even joy to the learning environment. The more variety you use in assessing students (summative or formative, written or oral, daily or at the end of a chapter, announced or unannounced), the more feedback both you and the student will have on whether learning is taking place. Also, using a variety of assessments will help students unsuited to pencil-and-paper tests feel successful.

- ◆ *Collegiality.* This is another vital element that is not part of a classroom but is essential to good implementation of differentiated instruction in any classroom. Collaboration, based on communication with other teachers or with consultants, helps everyone involved. At my school, those of us interested in differentiation took turns presenting to one another strategies we've tried. We have shared materials (maps, manipulatives, and even bulletin boards) and critiqued one another's ideas, looking for ways to implement methods or improve learning. Teachers, too, need connections, talk, open-endedness, and so on, as well as the feeling that we don't exist in a vacuum. (I've often heard foreign-language teachers say they feel this way.)

What Differentiation Is Not

Because graphics often help comprehension, see the compare-and-contrast table below.

Defining Differentiated Instruction

What Differentiated Instruction Is	What Differentiated Instruction Is Not
♦ Student centered	♦ Class centered
♦ For all students	♦ Mainly for students with learning problems
♦ For heterogeneous groups	♦ A tracking system by abilities
♦ A change in philosophy about how learning should take place	♦ A recipe for learning (it is how to teach, not what to teach)
♦ Multiple approaches or options for content, process, and product	♦ A different lesson plan for every student (individualized instruction)
♦ A mix of whole-class, group, and independent learning	♦ Whole-group drill and practice or any single structure or activity
♦ More about quality than quantity	♦ Fact-based learning alone
♦ Flexible and varied	♦ Unmanageable or undisciplined
♦ Proactive in the planning stage	♦ Modifying the instruction up or down in difficulty
♦ Rooted in assessment	♦ A method that you will need all new materials for
♦ Based on continual reflection and adjustment to help students learn well	♦ Cost free
	♦ Just about learning styles
♦ A belief system that says all learners come to the classroom with potential ready to be accessed	♦ Just a set of strategies and activities

Some Research to Support Differentiation

Differentiation was first developed as a way of dealing with gifted students, and most of the research applies to gifted and talented programs. Unfortunately, little research has been completed on the effectiveness of differentiated instruction in a foreign-language setting specifically. So, what we need to consider is research that focuses on the various principles of differentiation and their effectiveness, and studies that support those findings. Look for studies that show the effectiveness of things such as instruction based on readiness (Vygotsky, 1986), interests (Csikszentmihalyi, 1997), individualization, zone of proximal development, learning profiles (Sternberg, Torff & Grigorenko, 1998), attention to students' varied learning needs (Danielson, 1996) and, especially, effective instruction.

Let's start with the last one on that list. I first became interested in differentiation when, teaching on a block schedule, I sought more effective methods of instruction and tried to implement a greater variety of teaching styles.

My first contact with aspects of differentiated instruction was with Madeline Hunter's Direct Instruction Model (see Bibliography). Her essential elements of instruction are the following:

- ◆ An anticipatory set to introduce a new concept
- ◆ Objective, shared with students
- ◆ Input*
- ◆ Modeling
- ◆ Guided practice
- ◆ Checking for understanding
- ◆ Closure
- ◆ Individual practice*

The two starred elements above are key aspects of differentiation. Input, Hunter says, should come from a variety of sources: print, visuals, videos, and so on, chosen by the teacher for appropriateness (differentiation of content). Hunter mandates that the individual practice portion be used in enough different contexts so that the skill or concept may be applied to any relevant situation, not only the context in which it was originally learned (differentiation of process). Here is my favorite quote on the topic: "The failure to do this is responsible for most student failure to be able to apply something learned." (Joyce, Weil, & Calhoun, 2003, p. 312). She also strongly advocates employing higher-level activities through the use of Bloom's taxonomy model, which is also key in differentiated instruction.

Then there are the Cooperative Learning strategies of Spencer Kagan; these emphasize the importance of using learning groups, of flexible groupings, and of varying the roles and focuses of group learning, all important components in differentiation.

Joseph Renzulli (1997), who deals primarily with gifted and talented students, developed five Dimensions of Differentiation:

- ◆ Content
- ◆ Process
- ◆ Product
- ◆ Classroom
- ◆ Teacher

Notice that the top three dimensions are exactly the focus of a differentiated classroom. Renzulli also advocates many of the best practices used in differentiated instruction. In his discussion of content, he endorses exploring and webbing topics and using open-ended questions. For process, he supports using as many instructional techniques and materials as possible, as well as determining and motivating students' different learning styles. Under product, he advises a differentiated approach in which learners express themselves while applying the basic learnings of the content area. In the classroom, he envisions a combination of interest and learning centers, study areas, and work areas for artistic and scientific discoveries. He also advocates flexible group formats and an adaptable physical environment. For the teacher, he suggests that the instructor be part of the learning exploration, through the use of personal interests, collections, hobbies, opinions, beliefs, or enthusiasms about issues related to the content area being taught; this serves to spark curiosity or confrontation with knowledge, or just to model a love of learning.

The standards-based Dimensions of Learning of Robert Marzano (1997), the basis of constructivist theory, emphasize the different types of products that can be used to demonstrate learning and are well worth investigating for ideas.

Now let's talk about brain research, which I'd say has had the biggest effect on how I have modified my teaching (and the most positive effect so far on student success and pleasure in learning, in my opinion). Definitely check out the Multiple Intelligences of Howard Gardner (1991) and Brain-Compatible Learning of David Sousa (1995) for information that will change how you look at teaching forever. Both these researchers maintain that how students learn is shaped by their cultures and by their learning styles and intelligence preferences. Research supports those propositions, showing that student achievement benefits from teacher attention to students' learning patterns (Claxton, 1990, report on New York State Regents.) See Chapter 4 for more on this.

Preassessing readiness is an important part of differentiating. Basically, brain research shows that students do not learn effectively when tasks are too simple or too complex for their level of readiness. Also, for learning to occur, tasks must be moderately challenging: This is called the Zone of Proximal Development, or ZPD (Tomlinson, 2001, citing Lev Vygotsky, 1986). Vygotsky discovered that the difficulty of skills taught must be only slightly in advance of students' current level of mastery. Classroom research strongly supports the

ZPD concept. In differentiated classrooms where students performed with about 80 percent accuracy, they learned more and felt better about themselves and the subject area than before differentiation was implemented (Fisher et al., 1980, in Tomlinson, 2001).

Finally, brain and learning-styles research has also shown that addressing student interest enhances their motivation to learn. When teachers are able to make required content appeal to student interests, students are likely to respond with greater commitment, energy, and endurance. Research has confirmed that when students are engaged in what they study, learning outcomes are more positive in both the short term and the long term. Appealing to student interest is also an important component in differentiation.

A Few More Things That Should Be Mentioned

Effective management procedures, especially in the grouping of students for instruction, are central to differentiated instruction. These have been validated in so many studies (going back to the mid-1980s) that I'll not cite any here, but I will just mention that classroom management is an important consideration, and teachers should carefully think it through before implementing a differentiated unit (see Chapter 2 for examples).

Best-practice activities such as those already mentioned must be in your repertoire. Read up on some of the practices listed above if you're not familiar with them; observe colleagues using them, or attend workshops, and then work them into your own teaching until you are fairly comfortable with them. A list of practices often used in differentiation and definitions is included in Chapter 3.

Finally, a bit of personal action research: This year, in each level I taught, I deliberately differentiated the first half of one unit, including the assessment, and then used little or no differentiation for the second half. Comparing test scores, I saw that on average my students did 13 percent better on the assessment over the first part than over the second portion (on my grading scale, that meant an A– class average for the first test, and a high C average for the second). There were, admittedly, lots of uncontrolled variables (interest levels of students in the new material, ratio of grammar to vocabulary in each half of the unit, as well as the fact that I had already been teaching my students ways to use their own learning styles for success, and I'm sure that their having used those during the unit affected and improved their test scores). Still, I felt that an increase of two letter grades was a very significant difference in results, and confirmed my determination to continue differentiating in my classroom.

2

From Content to Process to Product

Differentiate What?	*Differentiate Why?*
Content	Readiness
Process	Interests
Product	Learning Styles

According to Diane Heacox (2002), differentiation is not too scary sounding: "Analyze the degree of challenge and variety in your current instructional plans. Modify, adapt, or design new approaches to instruction in response to students' needs, interests, and learning preferences."

There is no one recipe for differentiation, because it's not really a method; it's a way of thinking about teaching and learning that can be translated into classroom practice in *many* different ways. Still, there are some basic principles and characteristics necessary for establishing a differentiated classroom.

Content, or What to Teach

Differentiated content is the most frequently used (and perhaps the easiest) method of differentiation. Content refers to what I call the "big rocks" of the unit or lesson (see the story box on page 10). It is the essential information, ideas, attitudes, skills, or facts that students must grasp and be able to use. Students' access to content is the key building block in a differentiated classroom. There are several ways to differentiate content.

But first we must determine what content must be taught. I like to use the grid I received at a workshop for mentoring new teachers (see page 48 in Chapter 4), which asks us to "unpack" the curriculum unit into its component parts.

With content topic and goal now firmly in mind, we are ready to differentiate the content. One way is to use a variety of texts—simple or advanced, electronic or print—or text types, such as brochures, newspapers, music, poetry, ads, or menus. The texts used may be authentic or may be simplified or manufactured for student use. However, using a variety of printed texts alone is not real differentiation, because printed texts aren't accessible to all students (e.g., those who are dyslexic or who have poor eyesight or other difficulties with reading). Other resources that contain similar information include audio- and videotapes, DVDs, guest speakers, field trips, and Total Physical Response (TPR) or Total Physical Response Storytelling (TPRS). All this variety is often presented with a learning-center format (see Chapter 4 for concrete examples).

Another way to differentiate content is to give students choices in the type of instruction: direct instruction, concrete examples, work sheet practice, online work, or more complex activities. Differentiating content in this way requires pretesting (preassessment) to identify students who do not need direct instruction. The ones who demonstrate mastery on the pretest can go straight to the application portion of the unit. This is often called "compacting." This method is discussed more specifically in Chapter 4.

The "Big Rocks" Story

A story that has greatly influenced my teaching style for years is about a business teacher giving a demonstration to a group of students. He sets out a large-mouth mason pickle jar and a bag of large, fist-size rocks. He carefully places each rock in the jar, filling it to the top, and asks, "Is the jar full?"

The class nods, and he shakes his head and sighs, "No," and takes out a bag of pea-size gravel. This he pours over the rocks, shaking the jar until the gravel sifts into all the spaces between the rocks, and again he asks, "Is it full?"

One student timidly answers, "Maybe not?" and the speaker nods approvingly, and then pulls out a bag of sand and repeats what he did with the gravel. Again he asks the students, "Is it full?"

"No!" they shout, and he beams at them. He takes out a pitcher of water and pours it into the jar until it overflows. "Now," the instructor asks, "what was the point of my demonstration?"

"Oh," says the class, "that's easy. No matter what, you can always find space for a few more things."

"Oh, no!" disagrees the speaker. "My point is that if you don't put in the big rocks first, they won't all fit."

One final reminder: Content must be concept focused. A list of specific vocabulary in which every single word must be learned is *not* compatible with differentiated instruction. Activities (process) and assessment (product) enable students to practice and demonstrate mastery of the basic concepts, principles, and skills, not minute details.

Process, or How to Teach

Referring to the big-rocks story, content is represented by the different types and sizes of rocks. The steps taken to make the big rocks fit into the jar is what differentiation calls process.

- ◆ Process refers to how the teacher plans instruction: whole class, large group, paired, or individual.

- ◆ Process also refers to variety of ways by which students make sense of the content or input, and come to own it. Process should therefore appeal to students' learning styles.

- ◆ Process is also the use of a variety of flexible grouping methods: ability groups, interest groups, or learning-profile groups.

The most common method used in differentiating the process portion of a unit is to begin with a whole-class introduction to the "big rocks." The class then proceeds to work in small groups or in pairs and then uses graphic organizers, maps, diagrams, charts, and so on, in which students are encouraged to organize, seek relationships, and display their comprehension. Varying the complexity of these materials is an easy way to differentiate process.

Differentiating process means selecting a variety of learning activities or strategies to explore the concepts in the unit, according to students' interests, cognitive capacity, or learning styles. It is important to give students alternatives for manipulating the ideas you want them to learn. A day's lesson must not consist of drill and practice, or any single structure or activity. The difficult part is to make the tasks of each group equivalent. It is very important to work hard to ensure "respectful" activities for every student. There should not be a group of students that frequently do dull drills and another that does primarily creative work. Every task should also be productive and worthwhile, not busywork. Specific examples of each type of process are in Chapter 4.

There are three essential components in varying process:

- ◆ Preassessment must be done beforehand. Finding out where the starting point is will make a big difference as to what instruction or practice is needed. As stated in Chapter 1, skills taught should always be slightly in advance of the student's current level of mastery, so determining the level of mastery should be the first step (see examples in Chapter 4).

- ◆ Provide a balance between teacher-assigned and student-selected tasks. This balance will probably vary from class to class (even in the same subject) and from lesson to lesson and unit to unit. Giving students choices is good, but don't do it exclusively! This is especially true for language learning, as students might otherwise focus on the skill they are best at (listening, speaking, reading, or writing) and ignore the other three areas.

- Groups must not be fixed—that is, the grouping of students needs to be dynamic, based on ongoing evaluations of learning, behavior, and performance (such as how much effort is being made). Groups should be based on a chosen aspect, such as student interest, learning style, or performance on a preassessment. Learners in groups are expected to interact and work together as they develop knowledge.

Product, or How to Assess

Differentiating the product involves varying the complexity of the product created by students to demonstrate their level of mastery of the unit content. Products may be formal (like a report) or informal (e.g., an interview) and should be based on learning styles or multiple intelligences. Chapter 4 contains a Bloom's list of verbs as well as an Integration Matrix that lists possible products based on both Bloom's taxonomy and Gardner's theory of Multiple Intelligences. Chapter 5 also has a variety of products, and Chapter 6 has assessment checklists for many of those products.

Obviously, students with lower ability will be required to perform easier tasks, and more advanced students will produce work that requires more complex thought or more advanced accomplishments or tasks. However, it is also often motivating for students to be offered a choice of product. Because of interest in the subject, wanting to be with friends, or other motivating factors, students of lower ability may wish to join groups or do projects more difficult than those a teacher might assign to them. A good differentiated classroom would encourage this courage and determination, and the teacher might be surprised at what the students can do!

There are several key elements to differentiating product:

- Products should be accessible and challenging but should not overwhelm students.

- Products should emphasize critical and creative thinking as the students apply what they've learned.

- Products assigned by ability level should not penalize the advanced students: There should be something in it for them to choose to participate in at the higher level, whether it is an extremely exciting activity, less homework (but more complex thought), or required fewer activities. Students should regard higher-level participation not as a punishment for being smart but as a reward.

♦ Finally, products should be viewed not just as a way to measure learning but also as a logical outcome or extension of that learning. Students and teachers both should be asking themselves questions before, during, and after the creation of a product. Reflection is a vital component of the product process.

Preparing Yourself

Are You Ready for Differentiated Instruction?

How many of the following statements are true for you?

I love learning in general.

I believe in reading.

I value diversity.

I encourage student talk.

I say, "This reminds me of," and think aloud.

I revise and reflect on my lesson plans.

I try to grow intellectually and professionally.

I believe learning is a lifelong process.

I look for opportunities to get to know my students better.

I look for strengths instead of flaws and errors.

If you recognized yourself in three or more of these, either you are already using differentiated instruction in your classroom or you are mentally ready to begin doing so.

Let's see if you are *using* it now. The Self-Evaluation of Instructional Styles form on page 14 is a basic self-evaluation instrument you can use to rate yourself.

To score your differentiation readiness: The right-hand side of the scale refers to teaching strategies used for differentiated instruction. The closer your responses are to the right side, the more likely it is that you are already differentiating.

Your responses that are closer to the left are those that you will need to consider modifying in order to differentiate.

At this point, you may be saying to yourself, "I've been differentiating instruction for a long time; I just didn't know it!" Differentiation, just like any other teaching method, is based on sound teaching principles and a high-quality curriculum. Every time you give a student extra help or more time to work on a project, or modify an assignment, you are differentiating.

Self-Evaluation of Instructional Styles

Mark an X on each line according to where you think you are on the scale:

All students complete the same activities.	I give students a chance to select from a choice of activities, as appropriate, in a unit.
I use mostly whole-class instruction.	I use several formats: whole class, small groups, partners, individual.
I group students heterogeneously.	I group students according to their interests or needs.
I use similar teaching strategies from day to day.	I use a variety of strategies.
I assume my students have little or no knowledge of curriculum content.	I use preassessment before beginning a new unit.
Learning goals are the same for all students.	I adjust learning goals for students according to their needs.
When remediating or reteaching, I give more practice, using similar teaching strategies.	In reteaching, I use a different method from what I used the first time.
Enrichment or extension work provides more content or more application of skills.	Enrichment work demands critical thinking or production of new ideas.
I assess learning at the end of a unit or sequence.	I use ongoing assessment to check learning.
I use the same assessment or project for all students.	I provide a variety of ways for students to demonstrate skills.

Modified from Heacox (2002, pp. 19–20)

As a differentiated teacher, you will:

♦ Know what you want students to know, understand, and be able to do (key concepts, key skills—big rocks!) (content).

♦ Know a variety of activities that call students to practice those skills at different levels (process).

♦ Know how students will be able to show what they know (product).

You must:

♦ Use flexible grouping consistently.

- Know yourself well. You need to find your own, unique balance between differentiated instruction strategies and your own comfort level (based on personality, subject knowledge, or competency in teaching skills). Push yourself too hard, and you'll experience stress and failure. Think of yourself as a student of differentiated instruction: What is *your* learning style? Can you leap in, or do you need to test the waters and soak up things bit by bit?

Be prepared to:

- Give students a voice. Talk to them, and listen to what they have to say.

- Reflect on individuals as well as the group.

- Scrounge for a wide variety of materials.

- Build a sense of community in the classroom.

- Organize materials, space, and curriculum for essential skills and understandings.

- Diagnose student needs and strengths.

- Think of what could go wrong, and try to avoid potential problems.

- Share responsibility for teaching and learning with your students (and prepare students to share these roles!).

You will fail if:

- You try too much too fast. Developing new units takes time and effort. Gauge how much time you can put in without overloading other aspects of your life. Try doing some of the prethinking at a workshop on differentiation or during the summer break. Focus on one aspect at a time: Trying too many new things at once will make you feel like a circus juggler. Try one type of differentiation until you feel comfortable; then expand your repertoire with another. Rome wasn't built in a day, and neither is a functioning differentiated classroom.

- You let excuses stop you from trying things. You know, things like these: "Kids today just don't read; they watch too much TV," "No one enforces rules any more," and so on. You control what goes on in your room. Attitude and enthusiasm will get results.

- You do not reflect at the end of each day, and especially at the end of the unit, chapter, or lesson. Ask yourself: What went well? What went badly? How could I improve things? Make notes to yourself for next time you teach the unit.

Preparing the Students

Students come into your room already differentiated as to the following:

- ◆ Readiness
- ◆ Interests
- ◆ Learning styles
- ◆ Anxiety levels

The following display represents the various learning styles a teacher must take into account.

Student Learning Profiles to Consider

Grouping Preferences

Individual/independent/self-orienting/self-assessing
Peer work: partner
Peer work: small group
Mentor supervision (adult)

Cognitive Style

Big-picture ideas/specifics, details
Collaborative/competitive
Concrete/abstract
Creative/traditional
Inductive/deductive
Interpersonal/introspective
Linear/nonlinear
Reflective/action oriented
Social or people oriented/task oriented
Short attention span (easily distracted)/long attention span
Whole to part/ part to whole
More alert in morning/more alert in afternoon or evening

Learning Environment Needs

Quiet/noise
Still/mobile
Warm/cool
Flexible/fixed
"Busy"/uncluttered

Intelligences (Gardner and Others)

Right brain/left brain
Oral/interpersonal
Intrapersonal
Naturalistic
Analytical
Creative
Practical
Logical/mathematical
Musical/rhythmic
Existential
Verbal/linguistic
Spatial/visual

Readiness

To determine readiness, you'll need to preassess (see Chapter 4 for suggested methods). If the instrument you choose is not a self-assessment, share this information with students. They need to know their level of readiness in order to set an achievement goal.

Interests

Students generally already know what they are interested in; the key is for you to get to know their interests. There are many ways to do this, but the earlier in the school year you do this, the better. Some teachers hand around an information card on the first day and have students list their interests. Note: You can easily make this a game on day 2, by giving the students a Find Someone Who list. Later, you would take the interests from the cards and have students interview one another to collect signatures of classmates next to items they are interested in. You can also use the interest cards to make a nickname for each student in the target language; it can be a vocabulary-building tool or a way to introduce culture—e.g., naming a soccer fan "Ronaldinho" or "Victory."

I like to use KWL as a preassessment tool; the W portion will show me what my students are interested in. (See Chapter 3 for a definition of this vocabulary-oriented method.) For example, for a health or exercise unit, the words the students write under W tell me what sorts of activities they are interested in. If I have a whole class full of skater dudes, then I can bring in as much information on skateboarding as I can find online or in stores.

Activities like Four Corners provide motion and variety and help everyone to get to know preferences. In that game, each corner of the room represents a concept, and students choose which they like most by standing in that corner. Again, for the health or exercise unit, you could designate each corner as a season and have the students stand in the corner of the season in which they are most active, and then tell one another (and you) about what they do during that season. A similar activity, Lineups, has students literally take a stand on how strongly they feel about an idea (this also stimulates discussion and encourages the use of vocabulary words). Students line up according to how they feel about a topic such as vegetarianism (for a food or health unit) or the environment—anything they have an opinion about, including cultural content such as "I'd like to travel to..."

Learning Styles

I'd like to provide you with a little food for thought before we talk about evaluating learning styles, in hopes of convincing you that differentiation for learning styles is very important.

Calvin Taylor (1974), a researcher at the University of Utah, has developed the multiple-talent approach. He says that if teachers considered all the different talents present in a normal classroom environment, about 90 percent of students would be viewed as above average (gifted) in at least one area. The eight nontraditional abilities he names specifically are creative thinking, planning skills, the ability to implement a plan, decision making, forecasting, communication, human relations, and recognizing opportunities.

In his book *Little Geniuses,* psychologist Thomas Armstrong lists more than three dozen so-called unconventional talents that children have. Aside from the obvious (writing, mathematical, linguistic, etc.), the talents he listed also include the following:

- Acting ability
- Adventuresomeness
- Artistic talent/perceptiveness
- Athletic prowess
- Common sense
- Compassion
- Courage
- Curiosity/inquiring mind
- Intuition
- Inventiveness/creativity
- Leadership abilities
- Manual dexterity
- Mechanical know-how
- Moral character
- Musicality
- Passionate interest in a specific topic
- Patience
- Persistence
- Political astuteness
- Reflectiveness
- Resourcefulness
- Self-discipline
- Sense of humor
- Social savvy
- Spiritual sensibility
- Strong will/determination

Now, to those above, add 4MAT and Gardner's eight intelligences. With so many different talents, how can we *not* use more variety than the traditional paper-and-pen strategies?

So, how will you set about determining student learning styles? A couple of bits of advice:

- If you give a survey, keep it short.
- Tell students why you are doing this survey, and how important it is to take it seriously.

To help yourself and your students find out what their learning preferences and talents are, you will need to administer a multiple intelligences survey, like the one in the following display.

Gardner's Multiple Intelligences Survey

Name _____

Circle the activities you'd enjoy doing to show what you've learned.

Debate Write a brochure Write a poem Create a slogan/motto Make a speech	Write a research paper Write a summary Write a fairy tale or legend Take part in a mock trial Write a conversation or dialogue	Write a journal Tell a story Make an audiotape Write a story Design a checklist
Write a song Improvise music Perform a song Sing in a group Play a musical instrument	Write a rap Perform a rap Perform music Compose lyrics Perform in a musical	
Design a puzzle Create an analogy Make an outline Develop a theory Make a diagram	Analyze a trend Make a flowchart Design an opinion poll or a survey Evaluate or rate something Design a computer game, program, or graphic	Invent a code Draw a time line Make a storyboard Record dates or information Draw a caricature
Participate in a group activity Participate in a discussion Conduct an interview Paraphrase ideas of others Debate personal thoughts or perspectives	Build a group consensus Plan a campaign for an idea or issue Do a volunteer project Organize an event or activity Counsel your peers	
Draw a picture Make a mobile Build a model Make a poster Design a Web site	Make a map Design a postcard Design a greeting card Design a set for a play Make visual aids: pictures, props	Make a collage Create a cartoon Take photographs Make a sculpture Create a board game
Keep a journal Identify your beliefs about an issue Summarize your ideas and beliefs Present your own perspective, viewpoint, or belief Set personal goals Analyze or assess your own work Develop support for a personal opinion		
Perform a skit Make a video Do pantomime Construct a model Dance	Do a parody or spoof Perform in a play Develop an invention Dramatize a story or poem	
Classify objects Solve a problem Explore a topic or theme Create a collection Participate in a simulation	Construct a display of objects Make comparisons Conduct an observation Identify a problem	

Here's how each box translates into Gardner's intelligences:

Verbal-Linguistic	Musical
Math-Logic	Interpersonal
Spatial	Intrapersonal
Bodily-Kinesthetic	Naturalistic

After administering this survey and getting the results, I cut 3 × 5 index cards in half and put a student's name on each. Then I get eight different-colored markers and put a dot in the corner of the half card for each intelligence the student reacts strongly to. Then, when I decide to group students for projects by intelligences, I simply sort the cards out according to the colored dots.

You can view similar surveys online at:

http://surfaquarium.com/ MI/inventory.htm

http://www.ldpride.net/learning_style.html

http://www.metamath.com/multiple/multiple_choice_questions.html

http://www3.interscience.wiley.com:8100/legacy/college/strahler/0471417416/lss/survey.html

Although there is a connection between the intelligences and learning styles, they are not the same. The learning-styles questionnaire in the following display will tell you whether a student is a mover or a sitter; is an orderly, morning person or better in the afternoon; or possesses other, less conventional characteristics that contribute to success in learning.

Student Learning-Styles Survey

How do you like to learn?   *Yes*   *No*

1.   I like to sit at a table or desk to do my work.
2.   I like to work on the floor.
3.   I like to learn by talking to others.
4.   I like to learn by looking at pictures and reading things.
5.   I like to learn by moving or doing things.
6.   I like to learn by hearing things.
7.   I work hard for myself.
8.   I work hard to please my parents or teacher.
9.   I work on something until it's done, no matter what.
10. I work on something until I'm frustrated, and then quit.
11. I like to work by myself.
12. I like to work with a partner or in a group.
13. I like to have things broken down into specific steps on
     how to do an assignment.
14. I like to create my own plan for how to do an assignment.
15. I like to have a specific amount of time to finish my work.
16. I like to have unlimited time to do my work.
17. I like to work where it's quiet.
18. I like to have music or background noise when I work.
19. I am most awake and alert in the morning.
20. I am most awake and alert in the afternoon.

The answers to this survey show students' environmental needs, cognitive styles, and grouping preferences, as well as a little bit about their learning styles. This is helpful as the teacher chooses materials for study (e.g., if there are many visual learners, use more visuals and erase the board more often), gives instructions (e.g., break a task into small steps if the survey indicates a need for that), decides how much group work and how many noisy activities to do; it also gives the teacher a heads-up as to whether or not the class will be alert at eight a.m.

After administering the survey, I introduce activities, such as those in "How Should I Study," to help students see the best ways for them to retain information.

How Should I Study?

Find the numbers you answered yes to below, and read the advice.
(The more yes answers you have for one section, the more important it is for you to do.)

#3 and/or #5: **Auditory learner:** You like to be told things. In class, join discussions, make speeches, and tell stories. Read aloud. Create musical jingles to aid memorization, and practice them whenever you can. Study with someone else, and stop occasionally to talk over the information. Say words aloud to yourself. If studying alone (or during a test), imagine hearing the words on the paper. On a listening quiz, repeat the words very softly to yourself.

#4: **Visual learner:** You absorb new material better by seeing it. If there is a lecture, you *must* take notes, and add pictures when possible. Ask your teacher for printed handouts or more examples on the board. Sit where you can see the teacher's body language and face. Ask to have things diagramed. Use color to highlight important things in your notes. Seek out films, books, or articles on things you didn't grasp well in class. Make flash cards. Study in a quiet place away from verbal disturbances.

#2, 6: **Kinesthetic/sensory:** Hands-on learning works best for you. You need to see, hear, and touch things to learn them. If possible, do your work on computers or typewriters. Watch films on the information you want to learn. Use language labs that use both recorded and visual materials. Flash cards would work well for you, especially if you sort them into piles, using a system you invent.

#7, 9, 11, 14: **Work well on your own:** You can handle a big project or paper on your own, and do really well in areas that interest you. You may not need feedback while working, but you definitely need recognition when you are done. Celebrate finishing, and if you don't get recognition, *ask* for it!

#8, 10, 12, 13, 15: **Want feedback while working:** You work best on short assignments, and you prefer workbooks and assignments where things are broken down into small pieces. Ask someone for feedback while you are working. Break big projects into smaller pieces, and set deadlines for yourself to get them done.

#1, 18: **Mover:** You need breaks every half-hour or so. If you can't leave your desk, take a few really deep breaths, and alternately relax, tighten, and relax different body parts (especially your fingers, hands, and arms). Use bright colors to highlight reading, and before really reading it carefully, skim through it to get the general idea. Work while standing, riding an exercise bike, or pacing. Having posters around you is a good idea, and chewing gum while studying will help.

#5, 17: **Sitter:** Study when and where the only interruptions will be the ones you choose. Try to avoid clutter. This will allow you to absorb information without losing your train of thought.

#19: **Morning learner:** Try to schedule your most challenging classes in the morning, and don't start homework on Sunday night. Don't stay up late; set your alarm clock half an hour early to get up and review your notes.

#20: **Afternoon learner:** Take your most challenging classes later in the day. Also, rather than go home from school and turn on the TV, use the afternoon hours to do homework when you're at your best.

Other Learner-Classification Systems

The documents I've mentioned here are the ones I have chosen to use, but there are many different learner classifications. Following are some examples of common ones.

Right Brain/Left Brain

Experimentation has shown that the two different sides, or hemispheres, of the brain are responsible for different learning styles. Most people have a distinct hemisphere preference. The following chart lists the differences between left-brain and right-brain thinking.

Characteristics of Left- and Right-Brain Learners

Left Brain	Right Brain
Logical	Random
Sequential	Intuitive
Rational	Holistic
Analytical	Synthesizing
Objective	Subjective
Looks at parts	Looks at wholes
Accurate	Creative

Most instruction in schools appeals to left-brain learners. If you find a group that needs right-brain learning activities, try to incorporate more analogies and metaphors, patterning, role-playing, visuals, and movement into the classroom activities.

4MAT

I'm not at all a fan of this, but many schools use Bernice McCarthy's 4MAT system. It is supposedly based on a variation of the left- and right-brain belief and encourages the planning of activities that appeal to a variety of learning styles. She identifies four types of learners: innovative learners, analytic learners, common-sense learners, and dynamic learners.

- ◆ Innovative learners need to have reasons for learning that connects new information with personal experience and relevance to or usefulness in daily life. Some of the many instructional modes effective with this learner type are cooperative learning, brainstorming, and making connections with other subject areas.

- ◆ Analytic learners learn effectively from lectures and enjoy independent research, analysis of data, and hearing what the experts have to say. These students succeed best in undifferentiated classrooms.

- ◆ Common-sense learners need to do things. Using manipulatives, gestures, skits, and other kinesthetic experiences works best for these students.

- ◆ Dynamic learners prefer independent study. They also enjoy simulations, role-playing, and games.

One More Survey

As a developing differentiated-learning teacher, I've decided that I cannot know too much about my students. A useful thing to know about students is the so-called cultural capital they bring to the classroom. Examples of this concept are socioeconomic status, language spoken at home, parents' attitudes and expectations, support structure or lack of it, travel experiences, and reading habits. To effectively instruct a student, I believe, these must be determined and taken into account. I should be able to find out from the school guidance counselors about some of the cultural capital (especially socioeconomic level and parental supervision levels). But for less personal information, I've developed a survey that I began using last fall.

Cultural Capital Survey

Tell me a little about yourself.

Languages you speak (other than English)   Why you speak it:

_____   _____

_____   _____

Countries you've visited/lived in   For how long?   How old were you?

_____   _____   _____

_____   _____   _____

Types of books you read: (circle all that apply)

    nonfiction   science fiction   fantasy   poetry   biography

    mystery   romance   history   adventure comics

Other (explain): _____

How many hours do you read?   ____ per day   ____ per week

Do you have a computer at home?   Yes   No

Do you share it with others in the home?   Yes   No

If you have a job:

What school nights do you work? (circle all that apply)

    M   T   W   Th

How many hours do you work, in general?   _____ hours per week

Where do you work, or what type of work do you do? _____

What are your plans after high school (circle all that apply)?

    go to college   work   other: _____

Thanks for your help!

Explaining Differentiation to Your Students

Either before or after you administer your student surveys (I do it afterward) is the time to explain to students how you intend to use the information they have given you. Students have several needs (Tomlinson, 2002) that you should use to frame your explanation.

The first is affirmation:

♦ People here care about me, accept me just as I am, and listen to me.

♦ People here know how I'm doing and want me to do well.

♦ People acknowledge my interests and perspectives and act on them.

Another is power:

♦ What I learn here is useful.

♦ I can make choices that contribute to my success.

♦ I know what quality looks like and how to create high-quality work.

♦ Dependable support for success exists in this classroom.

The third that applies to the topic of introducing differentiation is contribution:

♦ I make a difference in this place.

♦ I help other students and the entire class to succeed.

♦ I am connected to others through mutual work on common goals.

Here are the key ideas I generally include in my explanation:

♦ Every student is different and special, as we've determined by the surveys.

♦ I want to help everyone to be as successful as possible, and I will use the information they've given me to design lessons that will suit them and their talents. I will make the assignments as clear as possible so they can do something they will be proud of.

♦ Sometimes we will all be working together, but often, because of the students' different talents, they may be doing different activities. A metaphor I like is that of a doctor, who prescribes different solutions for different symptoms.

♦ I want my students to be willing to stretch a bit and learn new things with me, without fear of put-downs from me or other students. I emphasize that I'll be asking for their feedback on things we do and that their success will encourage and guide me in helping them.

Helping Struggling Learners

As we all know, there are different types of strugglers. Some have learning disabilities, such as attention deficit/hyperactivity disorder or dyslexia or other handicaps (including those who should wear glasses but don't!). Others have such a difficult home life (e.g., having parents who are getting a divorce or having a chronically ill family member) that either all their energy and attention are focused on that or that they get little rest and are too tired to focus. Other students just find that languages require more effort than they expected or wanted. These are the ones that take all our energy, if we let them. Here are some basic principles for dealing with these students:

♦ Using the information you get from the student surveys, look for what the students *can* do, and design tasks for them that use those strengths. For example, a student who is kinesthetic (or has attention deficit disorder) should get a movement-oriented task, such as pantomiming a story as it is read. Make your students feel powerful and successful, and they will be more likely to participate. Give students as many different paths to reach the learning as you are able to.

◆ Make tasks relevant. If possible, make success at a task compellingly important. Work on learning-in-context, using authentic materials as much as possible. Things like "Ticket Out" (see Chapter 6) are highly motivating. Brain research tells us that simulations are the activities that produce the most long-term retention.

◆ Choose key, or power, concepts. If some students can't or won't learn everything, make sure they learn the basic big-picture things so they have a framework to build on when they are able to. Be clear about what they must know.

◆ Challenge your students. Don't make things too easy. Set a task a bit harder than they are currently able to manage, and then encourage, guide planning, reinforce criteria, etc. Self-esteem comes not from cheerleading praise but from the knowledge that we've made progress and done something that was a bit difficult for us.

◆ Give choices. Allow students to demonstrate mastery, using a method of their own choice. Sometimes students' interests might lead them to attempt something that you might have judged too difficult for them. Giving students a voice in what they do can make them more willing to participate, as well as more successful.

◆ Don't be afraid to show acceptance and a clear vision of a student's potential. Overlook the angry, bored, or sullen façade, and give students these two things that we all need, whether from a teacher or from friends and family: a vision of the good things they do and a vision of what they can become. This one is the hardest, and the most important, thing teachers do.

Management Issues and Ideas

Establishing Expectations

Behavior

This can be a problem in a differentiated classroom, if you don't set clear guidelines, post them, discuss them, and be consistent and fair about enforcing them. Everyone has his or her own comfort level for noise and motion in a classroom. But there are two important things to remember here.

♦ Don't have too many rules. Assertive discipline advises this one: Do whatever the teacher says, the first time he or she says it. That can really cover a variety of situations.

♦ Make your rules brief, and have students actually practice them. I am very strict about having students begin the opening activity (on the board or overhead) as soon as the bell rings. In addition to that, I use a timer that beeps for moving into and out of groups, getting workbooks, and other short activities, to get them used to getting to work right away.

Routine

Routine is good. Establish expectations for how and when to start class, and what the students should do if they finish early. I make sure every day begins and ends at their seat in a seating chart so I can keep track of students (especially on days when some will be in the computer lab and the others in class with me). Also, I always begin by introducing a new concept, so I need a signal to use to indicate that all attention be directed at me. Other routines and procedures to teach—and to practice—include where finished work should go and where students should go for information if they have been absent.

Independence

Independence is another concept to discuss. Have students help you list what an independent learner would look like. Talk to them about how you'd like them to call you for help (stay in seats and signal, come to you, etc.).

There are several other basic principles you need to implement in managing your classroom:

♦ Share your thinking/rationale with students (and their parents)—often. Students are usually responsive to a classroom that they know has been designed for them.

♦ Make sure you listen to their suggestions as well, nonjudgmentally. Respect and trust are really important. Students may have some ideas to forestall potential problems you didn't foresee, or ideas to streamline things, and your listening will foster an open atmosphere as well as give students a feeling of ownership for their classroom.

♦ Conversations about their experiences, frustrations, etc., will save a lot of time and stress in the long run.

♦ You need what Carol Tomlinson calls an "anchor activity" (Tomlinson, 1999, p. 32). This is an ongoing individual or group activity that will free you up to move from student to student or group to group. This also serves as a "sponge" activity for students who finish work early or who are waiting for you to get to them before they continue. Typical anchor activities are journal writing, reading (I have a shelf of little kids' books as well as a magazine rack of foreign-language magazines), an educational computer game, or practice papers, such as a folder of crosswords and word searches.

♦ Instructions must be very clear and precise. If directions are really complex, provide a step-by-step checklist on a card, or tape-record the directions for playback. Don't forget to give time limits, too.

♦ Make students as responsible as possible for their learning. Don't underestimate your students' capacity for self-governing and self-sufficiency. Use some of the techniques and ideas here to help this happen smoothly.

Grouping Students and Teaching Cooperative Skills

There are many different ways to group students. Sometimes I write a vocabulary word on the bottom of everyone's paper, and they seek out others with the same word. Other times I post a list on the wall, especially if the groups meet occasionally only but over a fairly long time span (e.g., my reading groups). As stated earlier, I may have "color groups" based on learning styles.

Teach students to work with a minimum of noise. Assign a student in each group to monitor the noise level and remind his or her partners to talk softly. Some students who need more quiet often choose to wear one of the listening lab headsets to cut out distractions.

Also make sure everyone is on the same page as to what on-task behavior looks and sounds like. Most differentiated teachers I know give students a daily behavior grade—a check for good behavior, a minus for needing a reminder, a check plus for extrahard concentration, and so on—and post this on a weekly chart. Praise goes a long way toward ensuring good behavior, as do rewards such as bonus points, candy, or whatever you feel comfortable with. Some teachers prefer to give everyone 100 points or pesetas or euros at the beginning of the grading period, and just deduct for bad behavior.

Teach students to move quickly and quietly into and out of groups. Practice a few times until they get it right and understand your expectations. It's time well spent.

Designate an advanced student or two as expert of the day for when you're busy and can't help or can't get around fast enough. I learned to do this when I had a crafts club, and more than 60 kids showed up. One person from each table would come to me to learn a skill, and then go back and supervise and teach it to their table while a couple of students with more experience and I circulated to help those who were really struggling.

Have signals planned. What will you do if you need the class to stop and discuss an issue that's come up, or get ready for a different activity? A certain spot in the room, a sound (someone on FLTEACH uses an electric door buzzer!), a hand in the air—whatever it is, teach the group. You certainly don't want to have to model bad behavior by screeching.

Creating a Sense of Community

Why is community so much more important in a differentiated classroom than in a nondifferentiated setting? Probably because there are more group activities, but the concept of community applies to everything that happens in a differentiated classroom. Therefore, you have to convince students that it is in their best interest to work, and work well, with you (you're part of the community, too) and with one another.

Several factors are common to groups that work well together (Etzioni, 1993.) The first—spirit—are the feelings of friendship and bonding that develop among learners as they enjoy one another and look forward to working together. Community spirit allows learners to challenge and to help one another. A good way to foster spirit is for students to find things they have in common. There are many party-mixer-type activities ("Find someone who…," Lineups, and others) that help students find things they have in common. Sometimes one of the roles I assign a team member is that of Praiser, who must give frequent compliments to each team member.

The second aspect is trust—both the feeling that other class members can be trusted and the confidence that they can rely on the others. Giving each group a simple cooperative activity they can do well together (such as a scavenger hunt in the classroom for information on bulletin boards or displays, following instructions by using manipulatives, or spelling alphabet letters with their bodies) helps students develop this. When we review directions (left, right, etc.), I blindfold one person and have the partner lead them through a maze created with chairs and desks. Not only do they enjoy this activity and really learn directions well; they look at their partner with more warmth than they did before.

A third factor is equality. Students must be able to participate as social equals (no bossy leaders) and as partners who have an equal opportunity and requirement to participate (everyone has an assigned role and is a part without which the whole will not be successful). Strategies that maintain etiquette and civility are good—not being able to speak without holding a certain object, for example. If one person dominates, give each person the same number of objects (I use poker chips found at garage sales) that they must ante in to speak, to touch the project, or whatever. When they are out of chips, they must let others continue the activity without their input, unless the group or teacher gives them permission.

Another key is that smaller groups seem to work better. For a reading group, I prefer groups of three. As stated above, I also assign roles that rotate: a leader or reader, a dictionary or resource for the leader, and a group secretary, who also handles manipulatives and signals me when the group has a question.

One other comment about groups: Research shows clearly that the most successful groups are those in which there is an alignment of teaching style and learning stage. That is just another reason differentiation is so good.

Tracking Task Completion

Usually what teachers are most worried about when they design a differentiated activity is how they will make sure students are on task, are following directions appropriately, and will finish on time. Here are some ways colleagues and I do this:

♦ Have students complete a daily work log in which they list their activities and progress for the day. This is a great anchor activity that is summative if done at the end of a class period, or a good reminder of where they were if done the day afterward (or you could have them reread the previous day's log to achieve the same purpose). Logs should be left in the classroom so you can review them. They are also, in the students' own handwriting, good evidence—for an administrator or a parent—of whether or not work took place (as well as of attendance or lack of it).

♦ Give all students a project checklist. This is especially effective with lower-level students, who generally need specific, detailed instructions. Breaking down assignments into smaller bits, each with its own due date, in a sort of time line can encourage students to stay on track for longer activities, as well as provide feedback that progress is being made and work has been successfully done. I've included several checklists for different types of projects in chapters 4 and 6.

♦ Quite a few teachers I know have for each unit a calendar on which are due dates for assignments, and a space for each day. At the beginning of a class period, a teacher has students get out homework and do a quick completion check, stamping or marking (e.g., check plus for done well, zero for none, an X for incomplete) in that day's square on the calendar. On page 33 is a sample calendar from Lisa Saragovia, who teaches at Mayfair High School in Lakewood, California.

♦ I often use another version, the tic-tac-toe menu (see the generic example here). It's also good to use for homework or when I'm absent;

it's an easy thing to tell the substitute to have them work on an item from "their grid"!

Tic-Tac-Toe Menu

Write	Speak & Write	Vocabulary
Write Exercises 5 and 6 in the workbook.	**Speak & Write** Survey five classmates about their likes and dislikes.	**Vocabulary** Do Activity 3 in your book, page 62.
Write Six things you might need to say in order to purchase food for dinner.	**Vocabulary** Make a game or puzzle to practice as many vocabulary words as possible.	**Speak** With a partner, one of you speaks a typical shopping dialogue as the other mimes the roles of seller and buyer.
Speak Create a song, poem, or rap that will help remember the vocabulary, and teach it to someone.	**Write** Make flash cards for vocabulary with a picture on one side, and the vocabulary word on the other.	**Vocabulary** Match the video and fill out the video-activity form.
Student:		Block:

The menu above is given to students for a foods unit for a skills-based differentiation of practice options. Students get to choose three activities that form a tic-tac-toe horizontally, vertically, or diagonally. Clear time frames are given for the completion of each of the three activities. (I like to have one due every other day, and these are generally done as homework assignments.) This method is useful for teachers who don't see students every day, as it encourages practice when not in the classroom.

To grade this, you need a special stamp and an inkpad. Tell students to get their choice of work and this menu out on their desks for you to examine, and while they begin work on something else, you can quickly check for completion or remediation and stamp the grid.

At the end of the unit, the student hands in this menu for whatever number of points you assign to it.

When it's time to assign a grade, a quick look at the calendar makes it easy to assign a grade, which leads me to a related topic: grading.

Sample Calendar: *Calendario Febrario*

Stra. Saragovia - Calendario
para febrero del 2005...
Unidad 2, Etapa 3

Staple your tarea libre coupons here. Write in assignment numbers _____

Apellido _____
Nombre _____
Período _____
Número de escritorio _____

FYI-GRADING
Participation 20%
Homework 25%
Exams & Quizzes 40%
Projects 15%

START THE NEW SEMESTER RIGHT! Do your homework! Have it ready and on your desk when the bell rings. See the teacher about tutoring if you are confused. Talk to the teacher about make-up work AFTER class!

PLEASE DO NOT chew gum, eat or drink, use makeup, write notes, arrive tardy, talk back, insult anybody or any group of people, etc.!
NEW DETENTIONS START AT 30 MINUTES!

lunes	martes	miércoles	jueves	viernes
7 Día libre - No hay escuela!	**8** CAHSEE EXAM FOR 10TH GRADERS	**9** 1. Preguntas personales, p. 143. Answer all questions in complete sentences.	**10** 2. Word squares due, "Activities, Places, and People and Other words" p. 163	**11** 3. Word squares due... "discussing plans," p. 163
14 Día de los presidentes No hay escuela!	**15** 4. Flash cards & vocab folds due for all words on p. 163. (No Coupons.) EXAMEN DE VOCABULARIO	**16** IR + A 5. Actividades 7 y 8 p. 149 and 150. (Just write one sentence for each number. Say what you are going to do when.)	**17** ER + IR Verbs 6. Actividades 12 y 13, página 152	**18** Irregular - YO 7. Actividades 15, 16, 17, página 153
21 Día de los presidentes No hay escuela!	**22** OIR 8. Actividades 18 y 19, página 155.	**23** 9. Answer all questions on pages 157 and 159.	**24** 10. Review packet due. Examen de gramatica.	**25** 11. Classwork - Movie Notes

Grading

With so many different activities, how can a teacher sanely manage differentiated grades? Here are some tips:

♦ Relabel the grade book. Instead of "Activity 6, page 42," call it "Practice 3/28" and list whatever work the students were doing on that date (March 28). Or label your grade book with the skill being practiced (e.g., reflexive verbs) and credit the students for their work on that skill.

♦ Every student should have a permanent folder that remains in the classroom, with a record-keeping form (such as one of the ones listed above) in it. On the form, students should keep a running record of work completed, date of completion, student or teacher comments about the work, and the work itself. Invest in different colored folders, tabs, or ink for each class period. An example of such a record-keeping form may be found below. Note: It will be necessary to clean out the folder after each unit. Those papers pile up quickly!

Computer-Assisted Translation Project

This exercise will help you evaluate computer-assisted translations.

Step 1: Research.   Due: _____

     Locate and use two computerized language-translation tools.

         List sources found:

         1.

         2.

Step 2: Try It Out (Part I).   Due: _____

     Translate the following pairs of sentences on each of the two Internet translation services, from English to French and then back to English:

The *bats fly* into the room.
The *bats fly* into the dugout when the *batters* hit too hard.

I like ice cream with *nuts* on *top*.
Some people think I'm *nuts*.

I *can* drink a *can* of soda.
Can you dance the *can-can*?

When I was a *kid*, I *found* a silver dollar.
On what date did Bill Gates *found* Microsoft?

If I *get* any more chocolates, I'll *get* sick of them.

Print the second English translation out, write "Source 1" or Source 2" on it, and hand in.

Which one did better, and why? _____

Step 3: Try It Out (Part II).   Due: _____

Write a one-paragraph autobiography in English in Word (name, age, family or friends, likes, future plans).

_____   Print it out.

_____   Choose the best translator from step 2. Paste in your English paragraph; translate it into French.

_____   Translate the French into any language other than English. Translate the product of that back into English.

_____   Print out the final translation (Eng-Fr- X-Eng).

_____   In a brief paragraph below the translation, compare the original version with the final English.

Step 4: Reflection.   Due: _____

Check all that are true:

_____   My teacher will be able to tell easily if I've used an online translator.

_____   Online translators do a good job.

_____   I might use an online translator for verb forms.

_____   I'm going to double-check anything I do on an online translator.

_____   This would really save me time while writing a paper.

_____   This was a useful activity for me.

♦ As above, students should do as much of the record keeping as possible. This will also serve the double purpose of keeping them up-to-date on how close they are to completing their work or the unit, as well as seeing the progress they are making. The extra column for questions or reflections will help them apply the metacognition that is so important to differentiated instruction.

♦ Consider giving grades for completion, instead of a formal grade. A musician may practice for hours on a piece, with his teacher's guidance and comments, but the assessment portion takes place only at the concert. Consider keeping track of who is productively engaged in working, and spot-check student progress with questions or comments as you walk around the room. This would also remove students' fear of making mistakes that would count against them and would stimulate intellectual risk taking. I always hated how the math teacher would tell us to read and practice a concept not yet taught in class, and then take a grade on that practice.

♦ Consider giving separate grades for different aspects of classwork. One category could be growth (changes from beginning of unit to end). I remember I used to get grades based on improvement of skills in physical-education class; this would also work for language class. Another category is standards-based achievement, for more normal tests and for quizzes that would predict success on standardized tests at the state (e.g., Regents), national (e.g., AP), or international (e.g., IB) level and for effort such as regular completion of work, staying on task, and contributing in class.

♦ Hold conferences with the students at least once during the unit. Ask students to help plan a project, set or evaluate goals, and assess progress. Sending the project record-keeping forms home is also a great way to communicate with parents.

Success and personal growth correlate highly with grades. Careful record keeping will help you and your students easily see their accomplishments and their success.

3

The Language of Differentiated Instruction: Key Words and Concepts

Academic literacy: Students need to learn to employ specific strategies to effectively read/use a text, and often these must be taught (or retaught). Examples of this:

- Studying the photos on a page before reading the page
- Using the dictionary portion at the back of the book
- Using the table of contents and index
- Reading headings and footnotes
- Looking for words in bold print or italics
- Using online resource materials to supplement the text
- Organizing data
- Reading maps and charts
- Evaluating the validity and authenticity of sources

Adjusted questioning: When a teacher alters the word choice and complexity of discourse or text to accommodate students' prior knowledge and current level of knowledge, he or she is using adjusted questioning. This is a simple way to differentiate for individual students or small groups within the same class.

Alternative assessment (also known as authentic or performance assessment): A performance assessment can be defined as any procedure that asks a student to create or construct an answer. An alternative assessment requires students to show us what they know and can do, in a meaningful, real-world application. Students know in advance what the criteria for their performance are and often have input in deciding what those will be. These assessments are scored on a point scale, based on well-defined criteria (a rubric), that is also presented in advance. Performance assessment requires students to be active participants who are learning while they are being assessed.

Anchor activity: A meaningful content-related activity that students can do independently, allowing small groups to meet with the teacher for differentiated instruction. Common examples are reading a book of choice, writing in a journal, and filling in a graphic organizer.

Bloom's taxonomy: This commonly known hierarchy is important to any classroom instruction, whether or not differentiation is used, but can be an important guide to teachers who wish to implement differentiation. In it, six levels of learning are established:

1. Knowledge of basic facts, vocabulary, or lists of things such as countries and capitals, plot and characters in a story.

2. Comprehension of concepts underlying basic facts, such as categories they belong to or how they work.

3. Application of information learned to a written or oral task. Examples are to write a letter, to perform appropriately in a simulation (speaking or listening).

4. Analysis of the structure or parts and their purpose.

5. Synthesis of learned material, with an emphasis on creativity.

6. Evaluating material and making a judgment about it, based on self-selected (or teacher-directed) criteria or other factors.

Many teachers often talk about "Bloom verbs" when writing curriculum or lesson plans, especially when writing tiered assignment plans. Typical verbs and activities for each level may be found in the display on page 59.

Choice chart: A list of choices of activities for students who have completed a required activity. These may be arranged according to types of activities (oral, written, listening), subject (grammar, vocabulary, culture), skill level (easy, more challenging), time frames, or learning styles or Multiple Intelligences. The Tic-Tac-Toe Menu (page 32) is an example, as is the practice grid in Chapter 5 (page 103).

Chunking of information: Brain-based research has shown us that we learn best by finding relationships, patterns, and connections. The best hook is previously learned material. Some visuals—such as graphic organizers, color coding, and certain types of PowerPoint presentations or videos—can assist students in chunking what might be otherwise isolated facts (especially spelling and verb endings). Chunking links the individual bits being learned together with previously learned material into clumps of information that the brain can process more easily—and that would be learned as an ensemble instead of individually—and is stored that way in long-term memory.

Clustering: Similar to chunking, this is a method of showing links between individual bits of information and the main ideas of a unit. It is useful for organizing information, especially for written work and also is an effective study technique. Clustering may show individual bits of information supporting a main idea or a main idea supported by other skills, principles, attitudes, or content.

Compacting: Examining curriculum to eliminate concepts, principles, or skills that have already been mastered. You would give a pretest, or use a survey or KWL (Know, Want to know, and Learned), to determine what students' true instructional level is. After determining which students already have a good understanding of a given concept, the teacher would give those students choices of (usually independent) activities for their class time while he or she brings the others up to speed. In my opinion, this is best used for short periods of time. This method helps to avoid boredom for more advanced students and gives the teachers fewer students on whom to concentrate for remedial instruction (see Chapter 4).

Constructivism (also known as active learning). This is the belief that true learning is not passive; thus, a constructivist teacher allows a learner to actively construct his or her learning focus or project, with authentic assessment, metacognition, and, usually, technology. Differentiated instruction is a form of constructivism.

Content, process, product: These are the three basic terms in the language of differentiated instruction promoted by Carol Ann Tomlinson (ASCD). These are explained in much more detail in Chapter 2. Content is the information learned about a topic, which will vary from student to student. Process is the method of investigation of and practice of that information, and product is the outcome (and assessment) of the process portion of learning.

Cornell note taking: A three-part system for taking notes that is highly efficient and helps students to do prethinking, take notes, and organize and process the information in those notes. This strategy is highly effective for some students in a differentiated classroom (see Chapter 5).

Cultural capital: This refers to the many aspects of students' lives outside the school environment that will affect their learning while at school. Examples of this are socioeconomic status, family (language spoken at home, attitudes and expectations, support structure or lack of it), travel, sense of safety, well-being, self-esteem, and reading habits. To effectively instruct a student, cultural capital must be determined and taken into account. (For a cultural-capital survey, see Chapter 2.)

Cultural literacy: E. D. Hirsch's definition of this concept is "the fund of information possessed by all competent readers belonging to a certain culture" (1997, p. 3) and the "shared knowledge that enables educated persons to take up any general text and read it...and to grasp the central message as well as the unstated implications of the underlying concept that give full meaning to what is read" (p. 4). Understanding anything in any language involves understanding the cultural context, an important component to language education.

Deductive reasoning: One of the most common methods of instruction, deductive reasoning begins with a general rule and then lists and has students put into use specific examples of that rule as well as exceptions to that rule. Spelling and many grammar points may be introduced in this way.

Depth and complexity: These two concepts must be considered when differentiating instruction for content. Depth is how much detail is used or how narrowly the concept is covered, and complexity is the number of steps, connections, or interrelated parts that are used. For example, the depth on a unit on health could be focused on learning to ask about or tell about general health (how you are feeling) for level 1 students or expanded to include health problems, such as illness and injuries, or a current food pyramid chart. The complexity could range from a variety of expressions from "Very good" to "Really awful" or proceed to different healthy practices, such as exercise and proper nutrition, as well as unhealthy habits.

Design-a-Day: This interest-based strategy lets students decide what to work on for a class period (or several). They specify goals, set time lines, and assess their progress. This is a good early step in preparing students for longer projects in a similar format.

Emotional intelligence: This concept (which is important in any classroom) refers to social behaviors such as self-control, communication skills, sensitivity to the needs of others, and other ways to function in social situations. Things like timing (wait time, for example), patience, empathy, humor, and ways of dealing with stress are examples of this intelligence. Emotional intelligence is not innate, as it was earlier believed, but it can be taught.

Features of differentiation: Differentiation involves any or all of the following:

- Pacing
- Structuring
- Learner independence
- Learning task

♦ Abstractness or concreteness

♦ Depth and complexity

All these are controlled by the teacher or facilitator and may vary greatly in quantity or degree. A differentiated lesson will have at least one (a learning task is the most basic requirement, of course) and often more of the above features.

Flexible grouping: With flexible grouping (which is essential to differentiated instruction), groups may be organized by the teacher or self-selected by the students. Groups may be formed according to interests or randomly but *never* by homogeneous ability levels. Flexible groups are often cooperative learning groups with assigned roles, such as literature circles.

Graphic organizer: Any kind of design, drawing, outline, web, or diagram that assists students to arrange information visually is a graphic organizer. Commonly used examples are Venn diagrams, flowcharts, semantic maps, or KWL (Know, Want to know, and Learned) charts. (Chapter 5 contains many other examples.)

Inclusion: This is a practice whereby students with special needs are mainstreamed into regular classes. Often, having such students means that a special education teacher or paraprofessional works collaboratively with the student and the classroom teacher to adapt instruction to the student's special needs. This involves a lot of training, common planning time, communication, and reflective practice, as well as administrative support.

Inductive reasoning: The inductive method of instruction begins with the presentation of a list of specific examples, which students organize and draw generalities from.

Inquiry activities: Often used in science, this strategy asks students to establish a goal or to state expectations or predictions before beginning a new unit, and then to self-monitor during the unit and reflect on the learning process and its success or failure at the end. Inquiry activities are quite effective for reading; Chapter 5 contains an example of the application of this method for a piece of literature.

KWL chart (sometimes KWLU): KWL stands for Know, Want to know, and Learned, the captions for this three-column chart or graphic organizer.

K	W	L	U

Using KWL is a great strategy when compacting. Have students write what they already know about a topic (reminding them of prior knowledge—which is great in upper levels when you're beginning a unit that expands on a previous year's learning) in the first column, K. Then have them write what they want/wish to know in the next column, W. As they write, the teacher can look at the students' work and see what they remember, and what sorts of interests in this topic the class has. This method also mimics aspects of the inquiry process and is a perfect fit with what an effective reader should do. As the students proceed during the unit, the third column, L, is used to record what is learned. A fourth column, U (for Use), is sometimes employed as an assessment piece for students to show what they've learned or to list real-life applications for the knowledge gained.

Learning center: For a learning center, various activities are scattered around the room at different stations. Students proceed to each area at their own pace, doing the activities found there. Centers typically ask students to read, write, listen, speak, draw, or practice in other ways material for a given unit. The centers can be student designed (turning the room into a museum, with each station a report on an artist, for example) and may present new information or simply practice information previously presented. (Examples of both are found in Chapter 4.)

Learning contract: As the name suggests, this is a *negotiated*, written agreement between student and teacher about what tasks will be done by the student and when the due dates for these tasks are, as well as the criteria for evaluation. A learning contract is used for compacting.

Learning style: This can be defined as the best method for a given student to process, remember, and use information. Gardner has eight (see Multiple Intelligence theory), and others classify students on a brain-based module: left brained or right brained. Bernice McCarthy's 4MAT system uses personality characteristics. A teacher who is aware of students' learning styles will be able to plan lessons and activities that are more beneficial to students (see Chapter 2).

Memory Model (also known as Link-Word): Memory Model is a form of mnemonics that is meant to make it easier for students to recall words by drawing from their own personal experience to form word associations. In step one, the students select the terms they must know—by reading and then underlining or listing unfamiliar words, by choosing the key points in a story or speech they wish to memorize, or by looking at a list the teacher has given them. Step two is to link the unfamiliar material to something they know, by several methods. To make the image memorable, the new idea must be sensory (i.e., using the senses, such as taste and smell) or motion oriented, perhaps very colorful or very exaggerated in size—in short, the new idea should be as creative and as humorous, outrageous, absurd, or downright silly as possible. Step three is to make it concrete: Draw a picture of this idea, making it visual as well as auditory. Then practice the associations to learn the vocabulary.

Metacognition: This is a psychological term for the process of learning how you learn things best (learning style).

Multiple Intelligence theory: Howard Gardner states that there are eight different intelligences, or learning styles:

- Verbal/linguistic
- Musical-rhythmic
- Logical-mathematical
- Interpersonal
- Intrapersonal
- Bodily-kinesthetic
- Visual-spatial
- Naturalistic

A knowledge of these styles and activities to appeal to them, as well as which of these are represented in the classroom, is essential to differentiated instruction.

Orbitals: This interest-based strategy helps students visualize topics of interest, devise questions to be answered, and then think of ways to share findings with the class.

Portfolio: An assessment that involves collecting samples of student work along with charts and documents that show clearly that the works selected for the portfolio are evidence of setting goals, striving to achieve them, and reflection on the process and results of the process of preparing the portfolio. A portfolio can be very creative and is an excellent way of organizing student input for a differentiated classroom.

Scaffolding: Scaffolding gives structure to learning and is essential for students who need things broken down into small steps. Graphic organizers, cloze sheets, dialogues, short-answer work sheets, and even crosswords (if not just a translation one, but one that might involve processing information such as putting on verb endings) may be scaffolding methods.

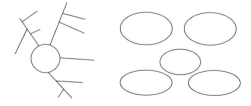

Semantic map: This is a form of graphic organizer for vocabulary and can be quite creative. A semantic map encourages students to think about what words mean and to categorize them. For example, in a chapter on adjectives, have students plug them in to circles labeled Size, Personality, Colors, and so on. Other organizers might ask students to show related words, synonym-and-antonym groupings, or gender groupings (see Chapter 5).

Simulation: This is a classroom setting in which students must interact with the teacher or with one another in a real-life situation. Examples are ordering from a menu, with students playing customer and waiter (and using real food, if possible), and following directions on a street map to find a given destination (or giving directions).

Socratic seminar: Student-centered discussion that encourages conversation and independent thought is the focus of a Socratic seminar. Questions have no right or wrong answers and no particular conclusions. (For example: If you met Cyrano de Bergerac or young Werther or Don Quixote, what would you like to ask him?) Socratic seminar is usually used for discussions of literature or films, but it is also adaptable to talking about national or cultural stereotypes and other philosophical concepts. The teacher generates the questions and ensures that students take turns and focus on the text or film rather than just express feelings not based on evidence.

Tiered assignment: Usually organized in three difference levels, tiered assignments are a method of giving students a choice in the depth and complexity of a task for a given unit. The teacher can use a preassessment to assign particular students or can allow students to choose. Samples and a discussion of tiered assignments are in Chapter 4.

Think-pair-share: Good any time, this is my favorite Cooperative Learning strategy. Students think of their individual answer to a question and then share it with a partner, and perhaps those two will share with another two people.

TPRS: In Blaine Ray's Total Physical Response Storytelling, students learn nine words at a time through gestures and practice and then gradually work them into sentences and stories, moving from oral or visual to written and reading activities. TPRS is a more recent version of Total Physical Response.

WebQuest: This is a teacher-designed lesson that uses the Internet to allow students, individually or in groups, to move through a process of researching a specific topic, drawing conclusions about it, and developing a presentation on it. A WebQuest can be differentiated for student readiness, but it is easiest to use as an interest-based differentiation strategy.

On the next page is a list of terms in this chapter, in reproducible form, for your own use (test your knowledge) or for photocopying for use in a collaborative learning situation.

Suggestion: Try putting these terms in categories/classification groups, such as "reading strategies." Note: This would be an inductive-reasoning activity, so it is best if you look for your own categories for these common terms.

Differentiated Instruction Terms

Academic literacy
Adjusted questioning
Alternative assessment
Anchor activity
Bloom's taxonomy
Choice chart
Chunking of information
Clustering
Compacting
Constructivism
Content, process, product
Cornell note taking
Cultural capital
Cultural literacy
Deductive reasoning
Depth and complexity
Design-a-Day
Emotional intelligence
Features of differentiation
Flexible grouping

Graphic organizer
Inclusion
Inductive reasoning
Inquiry activities
KWL chart (sometimes KWLU)
Learning center
Learning contract
Learning style
Memory Model
Metacognition
Multiple Intelligence theory
Orbitals
Portfolio
Scaffolding
Semantic map
Simulation
Socratic seminar
Tiered assignment
Think-pair-share
TPRS
WebQuest

4

Planning a Differentiated Unit

Planning a differentiated unit isn't hard. It should be very much like what you already do but should be just a little bit more intentional about catering to individual interests and using variety. There are only five steps:

1. Identify what is to be taught (content).
2. Preassess students' needs and capabilities.
3. Choose the form(s) of assessment to be used (product).
4. Decide on the method of presentation.
5. Select a variety of learning strategies (process).

Let's look at each of those in more depth.

Identify What Is to Be Taught (Content)

Start with the curriculum, of course. Then look at the teaching materials as well.

List the unit's "big rocks" (underlying concepts, skills, or knowledge—see the story in Chapter 2). For this, a graphic organizer sheet is very helpful. I like to use a form, such as that given to me in a mentoring workshop (see page 48), that unpacks a standard or a unit and makes you view it in six different ways. You can also develop your own form or checklist.

Graphic Organizer Sheet: Six Ways to Look at a New Unit

Standard(s):	
Declarative Knowledge Why do students need to know this?	**Procedural Knowledge** (Skills) What processes do students need to learn? *What should students be able to do years from now?*
What details must students learn? (Keep these to a minimum.)	What skills do students need to learn?
What necessary vocabulary terms or phrases are needed?	What steps or rules will students need to follow?

If you use a text, as I do, don't rely only on what the book tells you the goals are; your take on the goals is more important, because you'll be adapting the materials in the text to your own perceptions and teaching style.

Preassess Students' Needs and Capabilities

Review your students' needs. Our students don't come into our classrooms as blank slates ready to be filled with information, and the sooner we recognize this fact and deal with it, the closer we will be to reaching them and teaching them.

What student variables do you need to know for this unit that you don't know right now? These variables need to be considered in any instructional decision making:

♦ Readiness and skill levels represented in the class

♦ Interests

♦ Learning styles

♦ Anxiety levels

This is where preassessment comes in. Before you begin a new unit, do preassessment as a temperature check on the following:

- ◆ What students know so far

- ◆ What students need more work on or seem to have forgotten entirely

- ◆ Where students have exceeded expectations

- ◆ Questions students have

- ◆ Interest of students in this topic

Notice that I did not list learning *styles*, as that needs to be done only once, and not for each unit. For formal or informal ways to assess learning styles, see the discussion of this in Chapter 2.

Two types of preassessment are generally used: formal preassessment and informal preassessment.

Formal Preassessment

This usually takes the form of pretests, short quizzes, or students' performance or feedback on the previous end-of-unit assessment.

Mine your text's ancillaries and other supplemental material for pretests. For example, for my upper-level (advanced placement) class, I purchased a small book of grammar self-tests (*Harrap's French Exercises*) for my students.

A brief 10-point quiz (e.g., before a food unit: name a fruit, name a vegetable, name a dessert) will quickly help divide students into skill-level groupings.

Another quiz-type activity can be found online. I take my students to our Cyber Station and to a site, such as http://www.quia.com or http://www.fun brain.com, that offers ready-made quizzes (disguised as matching, hangman, word searches, and other types of activities) to allow you to monitor students' knowledge level while they review (or learn) vocabulary and grammar. These two sites do cost money to use—quia.com is $49 per year and funbrain $39.95 (but you can try them free for 30 days)—but they allow you to create your own material (including sounds and pictures), maintain an assignments-and-links page for your classes, and collect student results on the online quizzes.

A formal self-assessment at the end of each chapter or unit test is also a good idea. I include one or more reflection-type questions such as those in the following Reflection Self-Assessment display.

Reflection Self-Assessment

I feel (circle one)   *comfortable*   *somewhat comfortable*   *uncomfortable*
about my ability to (_"big rock" from unit_).

I thought it was easy to _____.

I enjoyed _____.

I was pleasantly surprised that I could _____.

I still need more work on _____.

I learned _____.

"Big rock" was   easy   /   not easy   for me.

Circle all strategies you found helpful:

video	workbook pages	partner work	listening to tape
rebus story	journal entries	verb grid	grammar song
reading	Internet	learning	Design-a Day
flash cards	other	groups	other: _____

I look closely at these responses, noting activities students found helpful, their perceptions of comfort with material, and so on. I also, of course, use their actual performance on the assessment.

Informal Preassessment

This can take the form of journal entries; written activities such as a KWL—Know, Want to know, Learned—(look at what they *Know*, which is written in the target language (TL), as well as the *Want* section in English, to determine student interests); webbing activities such as a Graffiti session, individually or with a partner; watching students during a game of Flyswatter/ Tapette/Matamoscas (using a flyswatter to demonstrate knowledge of words written on a blackboard or a poster or projected onto a wall or screen); watching or collecting a circle-the-correct-answer (alone or with a partner, each using a different-colored pencil or marker); having students signal their understanding with a Fist-to-Five show of fingers (fist is little understanding or comfort; five fingers is lots); or you can just base the preassessment on your everyday observations in class.

Anyone familiar with TPRS (Total Physical Response Storytelling) knows that you must choose a so-called barometer student in every class; the teacher watches this student for signs of confusion, frustration, or stress, and the student's behavior will tell the teacher to slow down, stop, and take stock of where everyone is, add more practice, or reteach the topic. Such students then go into the lower ability level, the ones whose hands are always in the air to contribute positively to class go in the advanced group, and the others go in the middle group or groups.

This display shows an informal survey of student interest (preassessment):

**Student-Interest Survey:
What Do You Want to Learn about Sports?**

What Do You Want to Learn about Sports?

Sports I enjoy participating in:

_____   _____

Sports I enjoy watching:

_____   _____

Sports I'd like to try:

_____   _____

Sports I'd like to learn more about:

_____   _____

Things I like to know about a sport (check all that apply):

    ___ Its history   ___ Its rules

    ___ Famous players   ___ Equipment needed

    ___ Records/bests   ___ Other: (specify)_____

What can you tell me about the following sports/events?:

    Pelote _____

    Canyoning _____

    Pétanque _____

    Fencing _____

    Tour de France _____

    The Paris-Dakar rally _____

    Le Mans _____

Choose the Form(s) of Assessment to Be Used (Product)

I am a big believer in teaching to the test, and I always write my test as the second step of preparation in my unit. I look at the so-called big rocks and devise a test that tests all the rocks and incorporates at least one section each of listening, writing, reading, and speaking activities. There are many different types of assessments: formal and informal, daily and end of unit, pencil and paper or performance, standardized or authentic. I try to use variety, but I do assess at least once a day, often at the beginning and *always* at the end of the class period. Once I have my assessments, I work on the next two planning steps. A discussion of differentiated assessments is in Chapter 6.

Decide on the Method of Presentation

How to Differentiate

Just ask yourself these questions to help you decide what type of differentiation will be best in these circumstances:

Do some students need more time to work on this, while others are ready to go on?

♦ Differentiate by process

♦ Differentiate by compacting

Are the students at different reading levels?

♦ Differentiate by resources

Do I want all the students to use the same materials, but produce different products matched to abilities or interests?

♦ Differentiate by outcome

Do students have many different learning styles?

♦ Differentiate by process

Would you like to have students make choices based on things they are interested in?

♦ Differentiate by interests

You want to engage all learners, as well as motivate them. After your preassessment of student interests, learning styles, and so on, use the criteria above to decide how you will differentiate this unit. I like to keep this saying in mind:

"What do you use to bait the hook? What *you* like, or what the *fish* likes?"

So, choose a hook (or hooks) for your fish. How will you introduce this topic to students? Determine what you will say to or show the class on the first day of this unit to introduce it. Here are some suggestions:

♦ At the front of the classroom, have a poster or an interesting object (African mask, drum, rain stick, jai alai or bullfight equipment, jewelry or pottery, and so on), and ask students to write down—in their day's journal or on a piece of scrap paper—a couple of questions about it or guess what the object is for or where they might find one.

♦ Tell students you've planned a guest speaker for the next day, and have them write questions for that person—and then you be the guest speaker (or have their partner, assigned by you, be the guest speaker: definitely good for a unit on the family!).

- Show them examples of a grammar point, and ask them to try to determine the rules for using it (concept-development or concept-induction method).

- Draw on students' own experiences by asking each of them to contribute to a list on the board of things such as favorite (or least favorite) foods, movies, celebrities (for a unit on descriptions or professions), or other category you're about to begin as a unit.

- Share a personal story or experience (travel, interest—I like to research the origins of people's last names and share that), collection, or hobby, and elicit input from students who do the same or similar things.

- Display both good and bad examples of a product and elicit input on what makes each good or bad.

Once your fish are hooked, you will also need to decide on your own presentation methods for the whole-class introduction of the concept, and for further practice as the class differentiates into different activities and smaller groups or individual work.

The following are some methods to consider:

- Hand signals, sign, or gestures (TPRS method)

- Repeating information, or asking students to repeat

- Involving students in the initial presentation. Anyone familiar with TPRS knows that the Personalize step is key to learning vocabulary. More on this in Chapter 5.

- Modifying usual tone of voice

- Writing information on board, on overhead, on Post-its, on students (washable markers when doing body parts is lots of fun)

- Demonstrating and modeling instructions (e.g., showing how to surf a Web site on screen)

- Thinking aloud

- Completing a first item with students

- Always putting instructions in same place in the room—I have an assignment grid on my board that students can look at, and I have rubrics for common assignments (e.g., poster or story) posted on the wall so that students can check their work.

- Tape-recording instructions (good for oral learners)

- Using visuals: pictures, posters, art, video

- Using different colors of chalk or pens (e.g., one color for verb stems and another for endings)

- Providing structure: activities such as fill-ins, graphic organizers, or Cornell notes while listening to an initial whole-group lecture

- Insisting on wait time before answering

- Color coding or highlighting key points (A recent study showed that when preterit verbs were written in bold, and imperfect in italics, students were more likely to use the verbs correctly.)

- Using team teaching—especially with a student teacher, a native speaker, or a colleague for an interdisciplinary unit

- Climbing the Bloom's taxonomy ladder during questioning

- Scaffolding for student work (especially for slower learners)

- Breaking everything down into smaller steps for slower learners

Classroom Environment

The method of presentation must take into account the classroom environment, as well as the materials to be used. Note these on the lesson plan or in the folder where you keep handouts and other artifacts to use for the lesson or unit.

Environmental variables include the following:

- Position of activity in the room—front, back, away from noise, next to the teacher, on the floor, or in the desk (I often introduce a new concept by having students move to sit somewhere new: e.g., a new seat or on the floor, or stand on a chair. This really wakes them up and calls their attention to the fact that something new and important is about to happen.)

- Lighting

- Desk arrangement

- Noise: music playing in background, talking only in whispers, and so on

- Class size or the number of groups

- Technology

- Need for movement around the room

Select a Variety of Learning Strategies (Process)

Once you have done the preassessment and planned your hook, it's time to design the lesson. This means you will now decide how the skill or concept will be practiced. Students should not just drill and practice, or concentrate on any single activity or structure. Remember that one size does not fit all; use variety.

Let's start: Choose any lesson you've done and remember well. Use the following chart: Designing a Differentiated Lesson. On the left, list the activities and strategies you used for that lesson. On the right, brainstorm (with a colleague, if possible) about how you could either change or rearrange the items on the left, and thereby differentiate the lesson.

Designing a Differentiated Lesson

Lesson as Taught	Possible Differentiations
Hook	
Introduction:	
Practice:	
Project:	
Assessment:	
Closure activity:	

Don't forget:

♦ Use Bloom's taxonomy levels (see the display on page 56) when planning the lesson.

How Bloom's Translates to Lesson Planning

Taxonomy Classification	Application
Knowledge	Requires memory only or repeating information
Comprehension	Requires rephrasing or explaining information
Application	Requires the application of knowledge to determine the answer
Analysis	Requires the identification of motives or causes or the drawing of conclusions
Synthesis	Requires making predictions, considering situations in which there is more than one correct solution or response, or producing an original communication
Evaluation	Requires making judgments or giving (supported) opinions

♦ List equipment or materials to be used (so you don't forget what they are and where they are).

♦ Estimate how much time each new activity will take. You don't want the new unit to force you to cut back on other curriculum.

♦ Build in at least one daily assessment to evaluate the effectiveness of the lesson. These may be any of the following:

  • Linked to method of performance

  • Linked to student learning styles

  • Linked to level of cognitive ability (Bloom's)

  • Linked to student skill level

See Chapter 6 for a more in-depth discussion of assessment methods.

To help you brainstorm, here is a list of activities grouped according to mode of presentation:

Whole-class activities:	Individualized activities:
◆ Brainstorming	◆ Application of skills
◆ Introduction of concepts	◆ Choice of task
◆ Planning projects	◆ Compacting
◆ Preassessment of readiness or interests or both	◆ Graphic organizer
◆ Sharing results	◆ Homework
◆ Socratic discussion	◆ Independent study
◆ Wrap-up of unit	◆ Interest centers
Small-group activities:	◆ Internet WebQuests
◆ Brainstorming	◆ Journals
◆ Discussion	◆ Memorization
◆ Internet WebQuests	◆ Practice of skills
◆ Jigsaw	◆ Products
◆ Literature Circles	◆ Self-assessment
◆ Planning	◆ Testing
◆ Reading	**Student-teacher conferences:**
◆ Research and investigation	◆ Assessment (several times during process)
◆ Sense making	◆ Evaluations
◆ Teaching	◆ Guidance
◆ Testing (see Chapter 7)	◆ Planning

Provide Scaffolding

Any good lesson must contain some sort of scaffolding. I truly believe students need to be taught how to *learn* a language, especially the good students, who are used to catching on easily and who have not developed some of the drill-and-practice skills of a hardworking lower-ability student. Scaffolding encourages students to become independent problem solvers and learners.

Scaffolding provides needed support for students to master a challenging assignment and maximizes efficiency in finding, recording, and examining what's important. Scaffolding also helps prevent students from getting distracted by details or going off track and thereby wasting time. It points them right to where they should go and what they should do. Sports Unit #1 in this chapter illustrates use of a scaffolding activity (see the display on page 75).

Here are the characteristics of a good scaffolding activity:

   ◆ Gives clear directions

- Asks essential questions (focuses students on basics, not trivia, in a reading)
- Because of this focus, guides work and minimizes nonessential work
- Keeps students on task
- Provides clear expectations of quality
- Points out sources of information and help
- Reduces uncertainty, surprise, and disappointment as to successful completion of the assignment

The following are examples of scaffolding:

- Study guides
- Graphic organizers (sometimes also called thinking maps, mind maps, power maps, or concept maps)
- Modeling
- Clear criteria (rubric)
- Checklists of tasks
- Icons to help interpret tasks
- Tape recorders to help oral learners
- Reading buddies (or writing buddies)
- Cornell note taking
- Manipulatives
- Gearing reading to student reading level

Most of the above methods are discussed in more detail in Chapter 5 and Chapter 6.

Bloom's Taxonomy

Bloom's Taxonomy is easy to understand and the most widely used classification system for learning activities. There are six categories (see the following display), listed in order from simplest to most complex.

Bloom's Taxonomy—Action Verbs

Use this list as a reference to see at what level you are asking your students to perform.

Knowledge	Comprehension	Application	Analysis	Synthesis	Evaluation
Remember previously learned info.	Demonstrate meaning of info.	Apply info to a real situation.	Break info into parts and see how they relate.	Rearrange info into something new.	Make judgments about info.
arrange choose combine compile copy count dance define draw fill in find hunt identify label list match memorize observe name play (a sport, an instrument) point quote rap recall recite recognize rehearse relate repeat review select show sing sketch spell state tell write on board	act categorize chart classify compare conclude correct demonstrate describe differentiate discover discuss explain extend find more about generalize give examples identify infer interpret locate outline paraphrase put into your own words recognize report research restate retell review rewrite show summarize visualize	adapt use apply build calculate change command construct convert demonstrate diagram display dramatize draw a map illustrate implement incorporate integrate interpret interview listen manipulate mime model modify operate order organize plan practice prepare produce record reformat reread research revise role-play sequence share simulate solve translate	analyze appraise brainstorm categorize choose classify compare connect contrast critique debate deduce dissect distinguish examine experiment infer investigate question organize select separate simplify solve survey test for	award cartoon caricature compose construct create design determine devise develop discuss disprove dispute explore hypothesize improvise influence invent make measure perform plan produce propose refine report rewrite satirize transform write	adapt appraise argue assess build change choose combine compile craft criticize decide defend elaborate estimate evaluate forecast imagine improve judge justify modify predict prioritize prove rank rate select self-evaluate suppose theorize value verify

Questions and activities for students should be geared for the higher end of the Bloom's list.

Chapter 2 had a discussion on assessing students' learning styles and Gardner's classification system. Here is a list of activities that cross-references the cognitive-level activities of Bloom with Gardner's learning styles. This will help you choose higher-level cognitive activities best suited to each student's learning style! I use this grid quite often when planning lessons.

Integration Matrix—Idea from Heacox, 2002; contents original

Gardner's Multiple Intelligences	Bloom's Taxonomy					
	Knowledge *Know it*	Comprehension *Understand it*	Application *Use it*	Analysis *Examine it*	Synthesis *Create it*	Evaluation *Judge it*
Verbal/Linguistic *Say it Write it*	Do puzzle Give examples, Matching or fill-in Multiple choice Conjugation Checklist Take notes (list) Menu	Put in context News article Spot "intruder" Retell story paraphrase Write biography Summary Survey Describe person Dialogue (read) Glossary Guidebook (read) Headline Job description Take notes (Cornell)	Speak, listen Postcard Book Letter Lesson Research paper Diary/journal Pamphlet or brochure Learning center Riddle Business letter Dialogue (write) Guidebook (write) Job interview	Questionnaire design Write a commercial Interview (questions) Comparison Metaphor Book report Movie review Discussion	Suggestions Story Slogan Ad campaign Poem Short story Radio show Play Critique Fairy tale PowerPoint presentation Creative writing, New story ending	Editorial Debate Panel or Socratic discussion Court trial Persuasive speech or essay Journal Interview script Petition Prediction Movie review Book report Award
Visual/Spatial *Picture it*	Read map or chart Acrostic Picture or video Film Detailed illustration Watch TV or a video Calendar Bulletin board Menu Draw flag Flash cards Transparency	Interpret a visual (chart, map, graph), Fix a visual Create a graphic or Mind Map Bullet chart Slide show Flannel board Weather map (read)	Build a puzzle Manipulate image Bulletin board Diorama Rebus story Job application Animation Blueprint Mobile Weather map (draw)	Compare and contrast (Venn) Jigsaw puzzle, Family tree diagram Mosaic Outline Pattern Stencil	Visual metaphor Design clothes, objects, costume Sketch or cartoon Paint Movie or video Puppet show Play Collage, mobile Map Sculpture Mural or banner Computer program, Pop-up book PowerPoint presentation Design a room, house Album cover	Award Critique any visual

Gardner's Multiple Intelligences	Bloom's Taxonomy →					
	Knowledge *Know it*	Comprehension *Understand it*	Application *Use it*	Analysis *Examine it*	Synthesis *Create it*	Evaluation *Judge it*
Visual/Spatial *Picture it*					Book jacket Design flag Mask wall hanging	
Logical/Mathematical *Count it*	Facts chart	Time line Flowchart Annotated bibliography Cartoon strip Bullet chart Pie chart	Connect or look for patterns	Solve Do experiment Graph Venn diagram	Labeled diagram	Ask questions
Bodily/Kinesthetic *Move it*	Dance Play sport Skit Observation Jigsaw	Demonstration Performance Play a game Prepare food Puppet show Charade Origami Move objects (Total Physical Response) Movement game	Mime Clay model Diorama Papier-mâché Make a map Simulation Card game Clothing Field trip	Taste new food, Compare foods (cheese, chocolate, etc.)	Craft Invention Sculpture Create a dance Make a hat puppet kite	Dramatize scene (video or audio) Express emotions bodily
Musical/Rhythmic *Hum it*	Recite poem Sing Chant Rap Play instrument Remember melody Choral reading	Interpret music Translate lyrics Transpose music Write lyrics			Compose music	
Interpersonal *Lead it*		Understand perspective/mood/feelings/motivations/intentions	Communicate (verbal/nonverbal)	Discussion	Plan a party, event	
Intrapersonal *Reflect on it*		Understand role in relation to others	Reason with self	Apply message/theme to own life written reflection		Self-evaluation
Naturalistic *Investigate it*	Read recipes, instructions		Bulletin board, scrapbook	Collection display investigation photo essay art gallery	Invent recipe	

You may use a blank of this matrix for planning purposes.

Integration Matrix

Gardner's Multiple Intelligences	Bloom's Taxonomy →					
	Knowledge *Know it*	Comprehension *Understand it*	Application *Use it*	Analysis *Examine it*	Synthesis *Create it*	Evaluation *Judge it*
Verbal/Linguistic *Say it Write it*						
Visual/Spatial *Picture it*						
Logical/Mathematical *Count it*						
Bodily/Kinesthetic *Move it*						
Musical/Rhythmic *Hum it*						
Interpersonal *Lead it*						
Intrapersonal *Reflect on it*						
Naturalistic *Investigate it*						

As mentioned earlier, Bloom's taxonomy is not the only classification system for cognitive activities. I was introduced to Williams's taxonomy at a workshop and was immediately interested in it, because it seems well suited to the communicative classroom style I am trying to foster.

Williams's Taxonomy

Fluency

As it sounds, fluency has its emphasis on producing as much as possible, quickly and accurately:

For example, "Write/name/identify as many _____ as possible in 60 seconds."

Flexibility

This asks students to handle unexpected responses, express themselves in an alternative way. The teacher can vary the size, shape, or quantities of input, time limits, and so on.

For example, classify the _____ listed in the exercise.

Develop a theory why _____ does this.

Originality

Students are asked to seek things that are not obvious, to suggest changes, and to be creative.

For example, think of a unique way to _____.

Write a new beginning or ending.

Create a graphic to express the concept of _____.

Elaboration

Synonyms for "elaborate" are "expand," "enlarge," "enrich," "embellish."

For example, explain what you think it'd be like today if _____.

Describe a time when you felt like the person in the video or story.

Risk Taking

Risk taking has students explore something unknown, take chances, and encounter new ideas and challenges to previously learned material or ideas.

For example, if you compared yourself to a _____, what kind of _____ would you be?

What would happen if you said _____ to a _____?

Curiosity

Teaching strategies designed to stimulate students by appealing to their curiosity have them formulate and follow a theory, inquire, question alternatives, ponder outcomes, and/or wonder about options.

For example, if you met a _____, what would you want to know about?

How do you think this verb tense is formed?

Which of these items is not an example of what we learned yesterday?

Complexity

After the teacher presents an assignment that requires multitasking, students are asked to create structure from chaos.

For example, describe or design an object or machine that could _____.

Create a new verb that follows the same pattern as _____.

Imagination

Students are asked to build mental images, picture new objects, reach beyond the practical and fantasize.

For example, imagine that _____ could talk. What would it say about (_____)?

If this author or character were here, what would you like to ask him, her, it? What might their reply be?

As interesting as Williams's classifications are, however, I have decided that they best suit only my advanced students, and—so far, at least—I have concentrated on using Bloom's, though I keep Williams's list handy for inspiration in creating upper-level cognitive applications.

Differentiating for Interests

One of the easiest ways to differentiate for interests is to provide a variety of topics. For example, in a sports unit, the teacher can provide information on three or four different sports, and students will select one to investigate.

Here are some commonly used interest-based strategies:

- Design-a-Day
- Exploratory studies
- Internet WebQuests
- I-searches*
- Jigsaw

- ◆ Learning centers
- ◆ Literature circles*
- ◆ Mentorships
- ◆ Orbitals
- ◆ Spin-offs
- ◆ Student choice of task
- ◆ Tiering

*Found in Chapter 5.

Here are some of my favorites from the list above.

Learning Centers

Also called interest centers, these are good for practicing previously learned material and for receiving new information at the same time.

To meet learners' diverse interests, align the so-called big rocks of the unit with topics that intrigue students, encourage them to investigate, and give them a choice of products or tasks, including student-designed options, in learning centers.

In the old use of these centers, the teacher created different centers and required all students to visit every one. In the differentiated classroom, the teacher creates a variety of centers based on assessment of learning profiles in the classroom, and assigns a student to centers according to the student's readiness, learning styles, or interests. Students are, however, free to visit other centers as well (self-selecting). Typically, they might be asked to visit a certain percentage of the centers before selecting one at which to stay for a follow-up activity. At each center, students should be able to work individually, with a partner, or in a small group.

A well-designed learning center does the following:

- ◆ Allows student choice
- ◆ Is motivating
- ◆ Satisfies curiosity
- ◆ Allows study of topics not in the regular curriculum
- ◆ Allows greater depth and breadth than the regular curriculum
- ◆ Can be modified for student readiness
- ◆ Encourages connections between the TL and either other school subjects or daily life
- ◆ Allows students with similar interests to work together

♦ For advanced learners, provides long blocks of time to work as well as more challenging work

Examples of learning centers are in the samples section at the end of this chapter.

WebQuests

A WebQuest is a great way to differentiate according to interests. This is an inquiry-based activity in which some (or all) of the information used comes from resources on the Internet. With a WebQuest, the teacher offers a variety of resources or topics as paths of inquiry for students, and provides students with a choice of tasks. Each student or student group is therefore able to choose a topic of interest and a task of interest while all are practicing unit vocabulary and skills. The first WebQuest I ever wrote was on the extreme sport of canyoning: http://www.msdsteuben.k12.in.us/dblaz/le%20canyoning.htm.

In it, students are first put into groups of mixed abilities and told their mission is to visit several Web sites and find out as much as they can about canyoning, to get permission to try it, and to get their friends to go with them. They are directed to a variety of Web sites and, as a group, fill out the WebQuest grid in this display.

WebQuest Grid

	English answer	*French vocabulary*
Who can do this?		
Opponent?		
Where? (What sort of environment?)	mountain	
Equipment necessary		
Optional gear		
Price of equipment		
Basic clothes		
Price of clothes		
Extra products sold		
Hazards or dangers		
Possible injuries		
Nutritional needs		
Training time		

Cost per session		
Action verbs used in this sport		
Useful adjectives to describe this sport		

Students are then asked to choose one of the following (each group member must be different from the others):

♦ Write a letter to the teacher, in French, requesting a field trip to go canyoning.

♦ Become an authority on this sport, and be interviewed, in French, by classmates about it.

♦ Make a poster in French, showing how the sport is done and its necessary equipment, and present this to your classmates.

♦ Develop a canyoning tour: Choose a destination, figure out what it will cost each participant (include transportation from the school, meals, etc.), and type up a brochure to hand out to recruit participants.

♦ Make a booklet of handy words and phrases for the trip: How do you, in French, say the things you'll need to say while you're canyoning? (Don't forget emergency situations; this *is* an extreme sport!)

♦ Write the speech that a guide for this sport would give a new group about to go out for their first canyoning experience.

Each underlined word above has its own product descriptor linked, and a grading rubric (the same for *all* the above projects) is provided as well.

Tiered Lessons

Tiered lessons begin with the presentation of a skill or concept in a whole-group format. Students are then put into small groups (usually groups of three work best), which begin to explore this concept in a "tiered" manner. There are four different ways to "tier" a lesson:

♦ By resources

♦ By outcome

♦ By process

♦ By product

The focus of a tiered assignment is for all students to achieve the same essential skills and understandings—but at different levels of complexity, abstractness, and open-endedness. Tiered lessons, like many other teaching strategies, are also known under other names, including layered curriculum and multiple-menu lessons.

Tiered by Resources

With this form of tiering, materials are chosen at various reading levels and complexity of content, and students are guided to those that will not overwhelm their capabilities. A teacher can also let students self-select. He or she might provide magazines, newspapers, brochures, books, online articles, videos, audiotapes, and so on; students can use those resources to find a predetermined number of something (and the number can be differentiated according to students' abilities): five authentic foods they'd like to eat, five examples of healthy lifestyles, five different regions of the target country that look interesting to them, and so on. Further resources might be a community mentor or expert, a native speaker, and other forms of print, such as poems, children's books, a play, and so on.

Tiered by Outcome

This is what is normally referred to as "tiering." With this method, each student uses the same materials (which is easier to prepare for) but as a path to a different end result. A basic group might simply identify the various aspects of a short story and make a Mind Map of the characters and events, while another might take a character from another story and say what he might have done if he had been in *this* story.

Tiered by Process

Sometimes you might want students to get a similar result in different ways. For example, a basic skills group might read through an authentic magazine aimed at a teen audience and look for what sorts of things teens in that country seem to be interested in. Another, advanced group could use the Internet to contact native-speaker teens and interview them online about their interests. A mid-level group could gather the results from the first two groups and prepare a Venn diagram comparing and contrasting their findings with American teens.

For tiering by process, offer a variety of assignment choices. A rule of thumb is to offer approximately three times as many choices as students will be required to perform. For example, if you want them to do five activities, you should offer 12 to 15 choices.

The layered-curriculum version contains C, B, and A layers. If students choose to do assignments only in the C layer, the highest grade they can get is a C. The B-layer students might earn a B (it's likely, though not guaranteed), and the A layer requires the most complex types of thinking. I do not recommend the layered-curriculum version, because it does not encourage students to excel, though it certainly offers many choices.

Tiered by Product

In this form, students are grouped by learning preference, and each group produces a different product (see page 156, a list of products based on Gardner's intelligences).

All assignments should be evaluated using the same set of rubrics, and the assignments must take equal effort and be appropriately challenging.

A Few Basic Bits of Advice for Tiering

- Teachers should use Bloom's taxonomy to guide them: advanced students will evaluate-synthesize, midlevel will apply, and so on.

- Start with the lowest-level activity, and design it first. Then develop the more challenging or complex activities. If the text gives a basic-level activity, use that as a starting point, and add a more challenging twist for the next level.

- Make sure your directions are *very* clear. Always provide a product descriptor (e.g., a checklist) for students to refer to in order to know what steps they need to take.

- *Always* keep in mind your big rock—what *all* students should learn (basic outcome)—and then think about what only *some* students will learn, because of difficulty, different interests, or whatever is being differentiated.

- Tiered assignments are a great way to do interdisciplinary collaboration with another teacher. Share the workload, as well as the benefits.

How Do I Make Tiered Levels Less Obvious?

I know that even in grade school, we all knew who were the so-called bluebirds and who were the starlings in the class. Here are some ways to help hide or lessen the distinction between groups:

- Label teams neutrally: colors, items of clothing. Recycle old vocabulary.

- Be equally enthusiastic about every group's assignment.

- Take turns introducing the various levels of activity (i.e., don't always start with the basic one).

- Make sure all activities are equally interesting and motivating.

- Unless you're tiering for learning preference, the assignment of every group should be equally active. Don't have one group use paper and pencil, while another does a skit or makes a video.

♦ All assignments should be fair in terms of the work involved. Think about the amount of work time involved, and make sure the time commitments are similar.

There are several examples of tiered lessons in the Samples section at the end of this chapter.

Spin-offs

Spin-offs (Heacox, 2002, pp. 109–110) can be done individually, in small groups, or with a partner. The teacher provides the general topic, and then students spin off into topics of their choice. An easy unit for this would be one on artists.

Choose a style of art and an artist associated with this style from this list:

Renaissance	Gothic	Baroque	Impressionist	Post-Impressionist
Surrealist	Pop Art	Abstract	Fauvist	Cubist

Include the following:

♦ Years when this style was popular

♦ Key elements of the style

♦ Biography of a chosen artist

♦ Works the artist is best known for

Products to share (choose one or more):

♦ Paper

♦ Illustrated time line

♦ Audiovisual presentation

♦ Poster

♦ News article

♦ Critique

♦ Scrapbook

♦ Original song or rap

♦ Storytelling

♦ Storyboard

♦ Skit

♦ Journal or diary from the artist's viewpoint

♦ A scripted interview, with the student playing the artist's role

- ◆ A copy the student has made of that artist's work, or an original work in the artist's style (students give a verbal explanation of what they've done and why)
- ◆ A PowerPoint presentation
- ◆ Other (see the teacher for approval)

A Few Tips on Doing Spin-Offs

Students usually select an overly broad topic. Break the project into steps, giving the students a planning-form organizer to record the resources they use, and narrow down the topic. Collect the form at various intervals to check on progress and give advice.

You need to have your evaluation rubric ready at the beginning. Have students attach this rubric to their planning forms and refer to it frequently as they do the research and prepare their product.

Compacting

- ◆ Certain students already seem to know most of a chapter at the very beginning or catch on really quickly. If you have some of those, consider letting them *compact out*. Here's how it works:
- ◆ At the very beginning of the chapter, give the final test for that unit to the entire class.
- ◆ Students who demonstrate competency on the test are allowed to choose and design an independent investigation or project to work on while the others continue the unit (a few may choose to continue working along with the class).
- ◆ Three days after you begin the unit, give the remaining students another chance to compact out.
- ◆ When the other students have completed the chapter, all students—including those who compacted out—do a mixed-group review and retake the end-of-unit test, to ensure that everyone stays fresh in the skills. As we all know, foreign languages are cumulative learning.

What Do You Do with the Advanced Learners Who Have Compacted Out?

I have my students choose units on an in-depth area of interest related to French. Some have done techno music, a particular castle, a poet, or a historic event. The students may work alone or in small groups. I have several forms I use to give structure to this; see the display that follows (also see page 162).

Compacting Form

Area above asterisks to be completed by student and okayed by teacher before beginning.

Student name: _____

Unit compacted: _____

Name of project: _____

Resources needed:

Steps in project:

*   *   *   *   *   *   *   *   *   *   *   *   *   *   *

Criteria for quality work:

____ Checklist completed

. ___ Self-evaluation completed

Method for sharing:

____ Display   ____ Presentation

Due date: _____

Another option if you would like more control is to assign a task (see Chapter 5 for ideas).

Interdisciplinary Possibilities

Differentiated instruction, especially when you allow differentiation by interests, will naturally involve other disciplines. Also, foreign languages by their very nature are interdisciplinary: we practice math when we learn numbers; research science in connection with the metric system and Celsius temperatures; economics with Web searches for various products; sociology in discussing culture; Family and Consumer Sciences when looking at foods; physical education, and sports; and so on. Jacobs and Borland (1986) found that students benefitted greatly from curriculum experiences that crossed or went beyond traditional content areas, particularly when they were encouraged to acquire an integrated understanding of knowledge and the structure of the disciplines. Small-group and partner work are ideal formats for interdisciplinary (and differentiated) instruction. Here is a graphic organizer that gives you an overview of how an interdisciplinary unit might be organized.

Graphic Organizer for an Interdisciplinary Unit

	Description	*Benefits*	*Considerations*
Webbed	Uses a theme or a major concept as a connecting focus for instruction.	Helps students see relationships and make connections between ideas.	Teacher must have the same students for several subjects, or teachers involved must have common planning time.
Interrelated	Same concepts and information are learned in several subject areas. Same skills, concepts, or attitudes are used in each area.	Helps students acquire and apply transferable skills. Motivates because students see connections between disciplines.	Themes or focus must be meaningful and relevant to students and to subject areas. Objectives of each subject must be included.

Several of the lessons that follow are interdisciplinary in nature.

Sample Units

First let's look at just *one* topic—sports—differentiated according to content, process, and product (to show the differences in how the unit might look). I'll follow up with several other units you could use.

Because none of these will be specific or unique to one foreign language, I'm going to show them in English, with work sheets in different languages whenever possible. As for textbook use, I'll just specify the type of exercise, and you'll need to look in your text for a corresponding one.

Sports Unit #1: Differentiated by Content

"Big rock": Students talk about sports they like and don't like.

Goal: Students select their area of expertise according to their interest and, using a variety of materials, research and present their sport to their classmates in the method of their choice.

Level: First-year students

Step 1: After introducing the unit topic of sports, have students do a Four Corners activity. Each corner of the room is labeled with a different category—for example, water sports, cold-weather sports, indoor sports, outdoor sports. Students are instructed to choose the corner they are most interested in and get out of their seats and quietly move to that corner.

Step 2: On the piece of paper below the category, have students list as many sports in that category as they can think of. Then assign the group to use dictionaries to find out how to say each word in the target language.

Step 3: The teacher presents a whole-class lecture on verbs frequently associated with sports (in French, *jouer à* and *faire de,* in Spanish *jugar* and *hacer,* in German, *spielen* and *machen*).

Step 4: Have each student in the group choose a different sport from their list and research it. Provide books, magazines, news articles, the Internet, a picture dictionary—as many resources as possible. Also provide a scaffolding sheet (as that in the display) to assist them in doing the research.

Scaffolding for Sports Unit #1

	English	*Target Language*
Name of sport:	_____	_____
Where sport is most often played:	_____	_____
Body parts used in playing: (as many as apply)	_____	_____
	_____	_____
Clothing to wear while playing:	_____	_____
	_____	_____
	_____	_____
Equipment needed:	_____	_____
	_____	_____
	_____	_____

Briefly describe the rules.

Briefly describe the sport's history (when and where it began, any other interesting facts).

What might your classmates find most interesting about this sport?

Step 5: Once the research has been completed, ask each student to prepare a presentation to the class in which they teach the name of the sport as well as five vocabulary words associated with it. For example, for basketball, they might choose to present the words "ball," "basket," "shoot," "dunk," and "dribble." They may choose the format for the presentation: a poster, a demonstration, a video, a brochure, an advertisement, a brief oral presentation of the six words with a word search or a crossword as a follow-up, a labeled diorama or mobile model, a newspaper story, a photo essay, a PowerPoint presentation, a rap or poem, or something they suggest. Have the students stay in their group's corner; they can rotate all four groups to give their presentation (small-group-format presentation is much less stressful for most students and has the advantage of making them present several times, for more mastery of their own subject matter).

Step 6: Give each student an alphabetized list of the sports to be presented, with a check sheet (see the displays on pages 77, 78) to fill out during the presentations, to assure their participation as active learners.

Step 7: To follow up, have students question one another about participation in the various sports and prepare a survey (written, bar-graph, or pie-chart style), a radio-news-style report, or a videotaped interview with a classmate about his or her sport. Another option is a "Find someone who…" sign-up sheet you would prepare after examining their check sheets. They find someone who skis, surfs, roller-skates, swims, etc., and interview classmates to get their signatures next to the particular sports on the list, which is in the target language.

Step 8: Assessment: "Ticket out"—at the end of the class period, in the last two minutes or so, have every student tell you a sport they do and one they don't do, in order to have permission to leave the room.

Sports Unit #2: Differentiated by Process

As stated in Chapter 2, most lessons differentiated by process begin with a whole-class introduction to the subject matter and important vocabulary. After that, students are divided into smaller groups to begin processing (practicing) the input they have just received.

Divide students into groups, and give each group a team name. Groups can be chosen according to any of several criteria. One division is by readiness: the students in need of remediation, the midlevel students, and the advanced learners. Another division is by learning styles; for example, you can use Gardner's Multiple Intelligences if you have tested the class for those, or LaMere's learning styles survey results.

Examples of both for beginning-level sports may be found on pages 79 and 80 .

List of Sports (French)

Sport	J'aime ce sport	Je n'aime pas ce sport	Je pratique ce sport	Je regarde ce sport
athlétisme				
base-ball				
basket-ball				
canoë				
canyoning				
escrime				
équitation				
football				
football américain				
gymnastique				
hockey				
judo				
lutte				
natation				
parapente				
patinage				
planche B voile				
roller				
rugby				
skate				
ski				
ski-nautique				
surf				
vélo				
volley				

List of Sports (Spanish)

Deportes	Me gusto	No me gusto	Juego	Miro
atletismo				
baloncesto				
barranquismo				
béisbol				
bicicleta				
canoa				
esgrima				
esquí				
esquí náutico				
equitación				
fútbol				
fútbol americano				
gimnástico				
hockey				
judo				
lucha				
monopatinaje				
natación				
parapente				
patinaje				
patinaje sobre				
ruedas				
roller				
rugby				
surf				
tablero a vela				
voleibol				

Differentiation by Process, according to Student Readiness Level (Tiered Lesson)

To give a little more choice, each member must do two items from their column as well as one from another column (see the display "Tiered Lesson"). This allows Group A students to do a project that interests them, even though it's not in the Group A column.

Note: Students are not explicitly told their group's designation (e.g., advanced), but in my experience they usually figure this out. The designations are based on a preassessment quiz.

Differentiation by Process: Tiered Lesson

Group C (Advanced)	Group B (Middle)	Group A (Lower)
Do Internet, magazine, or newspaper readings on sports; build a vocabulary sheet. Create a sportscast. Make a Little Book (see Chapter 5) of sports. Create a "team cheer."	Rebus a story on sports; read to partner. Create a PowerPoint presentation featuring classmates playing various sports. Video with graphic organizer (sports by categories). Give an oral presentation on one sport with a gym bag of props.	Label pictures of sports. Play a game of charades. Watch a video, and complete a work sheet of basic questions. Give a PowerPoint presentation on a sport of student's choice. Make a hanging mobile of vocabulary involving sports, equipment, etc.

Differentiation by Process, Using LaMere's Learning Styles or a Simplified Gardner's

After an introduction of the unit, and several workbook-type practice activities to determine mastery of the basics, students break into learning-style groups to do the activities for their category (see the display on Multisensory students). "Multisensory" students are those who tested equally strong in two or more categories on whatever evaluation scale you used to place them (and this does happen, especially in the case of really good students). The last activity listed is presented to the rest of the class for their enjoyment and instruction.

Differentiation by Process: Sensory Learning

Verbal Learners	Visual Learners	Kinesthetic Learners
Interview a partner or do a class survey of sports interests.	Go on a bulletin-board scavenger hunt (see the section "Creating a Sense of Community," in Chapter 2).	Play charades (students mime a sport and others guess).
Flash cards: make a group set with four one-sided cards of each word, and play Go Fish.	Flash cards: Make one set, the target language on one side and English on the other, and play Concentration.	Flash cards: Make one set, the target language on one side and English or a picture on the other; then sort into categories: by gender, by season, by where played, etc.
Make flash cards of only the words each finds difficult, and have them play War.	Use flash cards in the traditional way.	Prepare an exercise routine for athletes of a certain sport or create two cheers (with motions) appropriate for a certain sport.
Watch a music video that features a sport. Learn the words.	Watch the chapter video and do the work sheet provided.	
Make a skit of two people talking about sports, or tell a story involving a sport	Read and summarize articles from magazines, newspapers, or the Internet (choice of article and topic).	
Multisensory: Do one from each column.		

Sports Unit #3: Differentiated by Product

Version A, Using Learning Styles

After learning in detail about a sport of their choice (differentiation by interest), using a variety of materials (differentiation by content), students are divided by learning styles and given a choice of product for telling the class about their sport:

Verbal-Linguistic students (like to speak and write):

- ◆ Video
- ◆ Written report: paper, brochure, poster, RAFT assignment
- ◆ Oral report

Visual-Spatial students (like to see things, create things to see):

◆ Video

◆ Poster

◆ Little book (see Chapter 5)

Bodily-Kinesthetic students (like to move; like to physically manipulate objects)

◆ Poster

◆ Demonstration speech (gym bag with equipment)

◆ Flip book; read to a partner

◆ Mobile

◆ PowerPoint featuring classmates

All students, in mixed groups (one from each of the three groups above is ideal) are also asked to prepare, and lead the class in, an exercise routine (to incorporate commands, encouraging words, and other vocabulary associated with sports) that uses skills of all three types of learning style.

As a final assessment for this unit, a teacher might assign all students, in groups, to do one of these two choices:

◆ Create (using desktop publishing software, such as Microsoft Publisher) a sports page with articles on at least four sports as well as a health-related topic.

◆ Create a skit in which the students are sports reporters on TV, doing a broadcast (either live or videotaped).

Version B, Using Tiered Products for Different Ability Levels

Same instructions: Each person will choose a sport in the group's assigned category (see the next display). (Note: Category assignments only partially camouflage the fact that these are ability groupings.)

Differentiation by Product: Different Ability Levels

Group C (Advanced) Extreme sports (team sports, outdoor)	Group B (Middle) Winter sports	Group A (Lower) Water sports
Choose a sport, and create an imaginary team, with uniforms, star players, and a team cheer, and do a fake telecast about the sport and the team.	Choice of: Interactive (students make choices of what they want to see): Make a PowerPoint presentation that features classmates doing various sports they've chosen. Make a video report on their sports, with at least one athlete interview.	Choice of one: Make a Little Book on a chosen sport. Make a PowerPoint presentation. Make a video with basic information.

Learning Centers

Weather (Differentiated by Interests and Learning Styles)

Goal: To have students practice vocabulary related to weather at seven different learning centers appealing to different learning styles.

Method: Students select four different centers where they will practice different skills from the chapter. As they do so, they fill out a form, which they will later hand in.

Setup: Seven different learning centers are set up in the classroom, each using different equipment, manipulatives, and so on.

Cards
Computer
Television
Newspaper
Maps & Supplies
Tape Recorder

weather

Procedure: Students are given a form to fill out and told to select four activities. They are also told to proceed from one activity to another according to their own interests and not to stay with one partner or friend for the entire time. Students are also instructed to proceed from one activity to the next whenever they are done, and not to wait for another person or any signal, and to hand in their paper when it is completed.

Seven Suggested Learning Stations

1. A set of cards with the chapter vocabulary on them in English and in the target language (or, if preferred, with pictures of various weather, in photos or clip art or copied from the text in place of the English). Students should practice with these in one of two ways:

    *   Sort them into pairs and have someone else check and initial that these were done correctly. Variation: Have the students time how long it took them to sort the cards; then reset the timer and have them sort the cards at least one more time, putting down a best time on the work sheet, instead of having a partner or teacher check the pairs. (In this case, the teacher should provide an answer key of correct matches so that mistakes are not reinforced. Really low-level students could just use the key and look for the cards and match them up.)

    *   Place all the cards facedown and, individually or with a partner, play a game of Concentration. In Concentration, one player turns two cards face up and, if they are a match, moves them to a private pile, and then turns up two more at a time until the cards are not a match, at which point the partner (if there is one) takes a turn until he or she gets a mismatch. The winner is whoever gets the most cards in the pile.

2. A cassette recorder with a listening activity and an accompanying work sheet. Most texts have activities that could be used for this, or you could tape an actual radio broadcast in the TL (the Internet offers many possibilities for doing this) and you could provide a work sheet to practice listening to it in one of the following ways:

    *   On a map of the country or city where the broadcast initiated, students draw the weather they hear described so it looks like a TV weather map.

    *   If the broadcast is a forecast, students fill out a Monday-Tuesday-Wednesday grid with pictures or words showing the forecast.

- The teacher provides a sheet with weather expressions on it, and students circle the expressions they hear on the tape.

- Students get a cloze sheet of a script of the broadcast with blanks to fill in missing information: Tomorrow's high will be _____ degrees with a little _____

3. A television with a video clip of a TV weather report. A work sheet is provided similar to that described in activity 2.

4. A table with a map of a TL country, sheets of weather clip art, scissors, and glue. Students construct a weather map, using the materials, and then do one of the following:

   - Write five sentences, giving the date, season, and weather forecast for that day.

   - Show the picture to a partner (or the teacher) and describe the map orally.

   - Record a brief description of the map on a tape recorder provided.

5. A table with various weather maps cut from a TL language newspaper or from the Internet. (My favorite Internet sources for these are http://www.accuweather.com for maps with icons, or www.wunderground.com for a whole week's forecast. Both give the weather also for specific cities.)

   Students should tell what these maps say by doing one of the following:

   - Writing a translation of the information on the map (those two sites are in English), also using the calculator and formula provided to convert temperatures from Celsius to Fahrenheit or vice versa (math connection!)

   - Selecting pictures (or drawing pictures) of clothing they'd pack if going to that place for a vacation, based on the weather map

   - Making a similar map (labeled in the target language) for today's date at their school's location

6. A computer linked to a weather site for a particular country. Students draw the name of a city in that country from a box or a bowl full of slips and look up that city's weather. They then write out a weather forecast for that city.

7. A video camera and a wall map, a pointer and some props (rain hat, scarf and mittens, sunglasses, etc.) Students at this station videotape a weather broadcast that includes the date and the weather

(temperature and another aspect) for at least two locations on the map.

Evaluation Phase

Weather Assessment

Overnight I would assess these for completion and accuracy on a 1–10 scale as follows:

Name: _____

Activity 1	0 not done	1 done partially or incorrectly	2 done well
Activity 2	0 not done	1 done partially or incorrectly	2 done well
Activity 3	0 not done	1 done partially or incorrectly	2 done well
Activity 4	0 not done	1 done partially or incorrectly	2 done well
_____*	1	2	Total: ___/10

*These two extra points are for something behavioral such as neatness, cooperativeness, proceeding from one center to another in an orderly manner, or whatever aspect I'd like to focus on for that class.

(Note: I tell them beforehand the behavior for which I will be awarding these points!)

The next day, based on their papers, I assign students one of three different homework assignments from the book or supplementary materials based on their mastery level shown during the learning centers.

Classroom Museum

This is not a teacher-generated learning center, but rather, the format I use for students to give reports on cultural topics. It's much less intimidating than standing before an entire class, and more hands-on than just listening and taking notes. It also requires the student giving the report to give it more than once, usually resulting in a rather polished presentation (by the third or fourth repetition) as well as long-term memory on their part of the particulars for their own topic.

Students select a topic of their own choosing (though I don't allow duplicate reports), do research and then prepare reports, an audiovisual, and a manipulative for their subject. The subject usually is a Francophone (French-speaking) country or a Paris monument for Level 1, a famous French person or region of France for Level 2, or an artist for Level 5. Here are some examples of audiovisuals and manipulatives to go with a printed report:

Reports

♦ Standard school report, written in sentence form, double-spaced and in at least size-16 typeface (I have lots of students who should wear glasses and do not!)

◆ Brochure about the topic prepared by the student. Microsoft Office has a good brochure master for doing this.

◆ Children's storybook (can be comic book format) about this topic, prepared by student.

◆ Narrative storyboard (pictures with labels and/or dialogue)

Audiovisuals

◆ Poster

◆ PowerPoint on disk (so we can use laptops in situations of multiple presentations on the same day)

◆ Videotape

◆ Audiotape

◆ Original artwork or collage

◆ A T-shirt (made by student) that displays a variety of information about the topic

◆ A brochure from or about the topic, obtained from a tourism site, museum, etc., by writing to or visiting that place

Manipulatives

(See Chapter 5 for instructions on making some of these items.)

◆ Lift-the-flap sheet (with either a question on the flap and the answer below or a picture on the flap with a description below)

◆ A jigsaw puzzle of the country or a monument or a painting by the artist, with a picture on one side and information on the back, broken apart and ready for assembly

◆ A flip book or a Little Book

◆ A suitcase full of labeled items that represent some aspect of the report topic. Students unpack the suitcase, read each item, and then repack it. With prior teacher approval, some suitcases may also contain edible items for students to try.

◆ A board game

(Note: There are rubrics for many of the above projects in Chapter 6.)

Procedure

◆ Not all students will present each day. In a class of 25, we generally have five "museum"-format presentations, in which five students present their work.

♦ Students who visit each learning center should do two of the three things provided: read the report, look at an audiovisual, or do a manipulative activity. They must also ask a question of the student who did the report.

♦ All students are provided with a graphic organizer to take notes for an eventual test on these reports, and are expected to take notes while touring the museum.

♦ In upper-level classes, all talking (with the exception of an occasional, accidental "wow!" or other such exclamation) is done in the target language. Because my main objective is for them to learn the culture in the lower-level classes, I'm more realistic in allowing them to pretend they're in a foreign museum: Everything is in the target language, but the students can talk about it in their native language.

Interdisciplinary Units

Literature: The Hunchback of Notre Dame

Differentiated by Interests

This unit is done before the class views the movie named above and is presented in a jigsaw format (i.e., groups with one person from each interest "satellite" will take turns telling about their group's findings) as students do a show-what-you-know presentation that the teacher can use as an assessment.

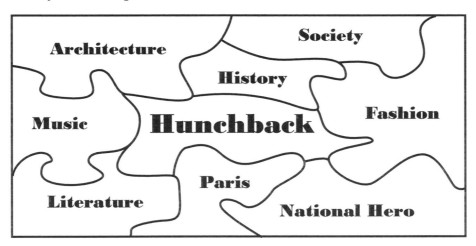

♦ **Architecture:** Look at the pages marked in the art books, and list the characteristics of medieval architecture on the sheet provided.

♦ **History:** Use the Internet to find information on the historical events listed on the time line at this center. Write a brief description next to each item (e.g., "war," "law," "king") What event do you find most interesting?

♦ **Literature:** The writer in the movie is similar to the poet François Villon. Find out his life story as well as what he wrote about. Find an English translation of his "Ballad of Hanged Men," and discuss it.

♦ **Music:** Listen to the music on the tape provided. Draw a picture or write a poem or story of what it sounds like. While watching the movie, note where and when it's used.

♦ **Society:** Read the two articles provided. Who are the Gypsies? How and why were they disliked or discriminated against? Is it still the case today?

♦ **Fashion:** Look through the books provided and explore the fashions for women and men, both rich and poor, for this time period. Be ready to describe this for classmates. If possible, make some drawings to share or show.

♦ **Paris:** Go on the Internet and look at maps of medieval Paris. How big was it? Who lived there? What were its main buildings? Print out a map you like, and be ready to describe it to classmates.

♦ **Hero:** Read the short biography of the author, and see what his beliefs were and how this book affected his life.

Show-what-you-know assessment:

Your group will create one of the following for *The Hunchback of Notre Dame*:

♦ A movie poster with one visual from each person's report

♦ A mobile with one element from each report topic

♦ A poem with at least one line from each expert in the group

♦ A rap or song with one contribution from each area

♦ Other (see teacher for approval)

Due date: _____

Valentines—An Interdisciplinary Unit

This unit has connections to: geography, fine arts, journalism, health, sociology, and FACS.

Lookin' for love in all sorts of places

Pick a country from the list provided. Using the Internet, do five of the following:

- ◆ Find out how to say words associated with love in the target language (including verbs and phrases used to say you love someone or something). Make a list of these words and their translation.
- ◆ Find out what symbols are used or associated with love.
- ◆ How is courtship conducted?
- ◆ How is Valentine's Day celebrated there?
- ◆ What is a typical marriage ceremony like?
- ◆ Is love typically associated with marriage? How?
- ◆ What sorts of love poetry has been written in this country? Find a poem typical of this country or of one of the cultures in this country.

Final Projects

Level 1: Do two of the following:

- ◆ Use five of the vocabulary words you found to make a Valentine.
- ◆ Make a poster with ten vocabulary words on it, and an illustration for each.
- ◆ Make a Little Book about love in "your" country.
- ◆ Write a poem or rap about what you found interesting about your research.
- ◆ What foods are traditional in this country? Describe a meal a loving mother might prepare for her family, or interview students in that country via the Internet to find out their favorite foods.

Level 2: Do one of the above, and one from the list below:

♦ Make a poster showing a typical family (or the royal family) in this country.

♦ Use the Internet to interview students in their country about romantic experiences, and write a short article for the class to read. (Keep it school-appropriate!)

♦ Find drawings, paintings, statues, and so on, from your country that depict love. Write a short statement about each.

Level 3: Do one of any of the above, and one from the list below:

♦ Write a skit, a play, or a readers theater script about a romance in this country.

♦ Use a camera to create a PowerPoint presentation or a photo journal of love around you. Be creative in your choices. Label or narrate your pictures.

♦ Write two love poems of your own, using vocabulary from your investigation. They need not be about a person. You can love an object, an activity, or a place.

Differentiation by Choice or Interests

Cultural Adventure Unit:
Language in Our Community (Spanish)

Level: Elementary or Year 1

Have students pick a destination and do the appropriate prethinking portion of the work sheet and then visit the location, as a class field trip or as homework, with a parent or a friend. If the latter, have the students get a signature from an employee there to verify the information. Then in class have students do the reflection portion.

Grocery Store

Hand in to teacher *before* the visit   Appellido_____

Where are you going to visit? _____

Date of visit: _____

What items and products from Spanish-speaking countries do you expect to find there?

List each under the section where you will look for it.

Fruits and vegetables (produce) Item Price	Frozen foods Item Price
Crackers and snacks Item Price	Bakery Item Price
Other: Item Price	
During your visit: Put a check mark on the items above that you found, and write the price. Then list other items you found that were not on your list.	

Signature of store employee: _____

Reflection:

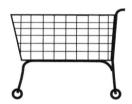

   Talk to other students or groups. List two items they
   found that you did not look for or did not find:

   Were you surprised at how much you found?
   Explain.

   Extra credit: Buy a product, try it, and tell me about it below.

   More extra credit: Buy a product and share it with the class!

   Note: This assignment type also works really well at the following:

   ◆ Record stores (Spanish)

   ◆ Movie-rental stores (Spanish or French, a few German movies some-
     times)

   ◆ Online (Students can shop online for clothing and groceries, check
     out movies, and find other products of the target culture and fill out
     similar forms.)

Tiered Lesson Plans

Clothing (Tiered by Product)

Targeted standards:

- ♦ Communication (presentational mode)
- ♦ Cultures (products and perspectives)
- ♦ Connections (accessing information)
- ♦ Comparisons (cultural comparison)
- ♦ Communities (within and beyond the school)

After an initial presentation of vocabulary via text, students are preassessed and assigned to a tier but are allowed to self-select the assignment if they would like to change groups, and they may work alone or with a partner.

Tier 1 (Complex/Abstract)

Your role is to write two role-playing scenarios for employees of a clothing store to use in practicing how to deal with a variety of customers. In each, set up practice conversations between two difficult customers and a salesperson. The salesperson should encourage and persuade the customers, rather than be confrontational. One customer should complain about price, and another about size or color.

Submit a written copy, and be ready to present as a model your favorite scenario of the two you've written.

Tier 2 (Midrange)

Your role is to write dress code rules for school. Describe at least six types of clothes that are acceptable, and at least six that aren't. Turn in a neatly written copy of the rules for approval, and then create a poster of fashion do's and don'ts, and be ready to present it to the class.

Tier 3 (Concrete)

You work for an ad agency and have been assigned to create a mini-catalog or a brochure for the big sale next weekend at a department store. Using magazine pictures, authentic photos from the Internet (see the teacher for recommended sites), or your own drawings, create your sale flyer. You can decide the theme (e.g., sport clothes), age, or gender group to target. There must be at least 12 items, priced in euros. Make the ad as appealing and creative as possible, and be ready to present the ad to the class.

On the due date for the products, I will use a jigsaw presentation method (students present to small groups of students and move from group to group to repeat their presentations).

Tiered Lesson: Numbers 0–100 (Tiered by Process)

Note: Students are asked to do all levels. Students who complete the synthesis level receive a C, the application level a B, and the mastery level get an A. This activity is patterned after several I saw in books on differentiation but is not one I've used personally.

Synthesis Level

Do activities to total 65 points (points are listed after activities).

♦ Create flash cards for numbers from 0 to 31. (10)

♦ Create flash cards by fives, from 5 to 100. (10)

♦ Write a five-question math work sheet, spelling out all numbers, and have three other students complete it. Grade their work and return it to the students for them to see; then re-collect the sheets and staple them together. (10)

♦ Make a numbers word search and have three classmates do it. Do not write out the numbers—use numerals as your clues. (10)

♦ Do up to four math work sheets (made by students, or get one from teacher) (5 points per work sheet).

♦ Design a poster or make a mobile, using the words for at least 10 numbers from zero to 100. (10)

♦ Listen and repeat the numbers on the CD track #_____ (page _____ in book). (5)

♦ Do exercise _____ on page _____. (5)

♦ Write and act out a short skit, using numbers. Perform it for an audience of at least three other students. (10)

♦ Find, print out, and show an article from the Internet with numbers written out in (target language). Highlight all the number words. (5)

♦ With at least one partner, toss a Beanbag or play patty-cake to recite numbers for at least five minutes. (5)

♦ Tell the teacher your book number, locker number, or zip code in (target language). (5 points each)

♦ Jump rope and count in (target language) for at least 5 minutes. Whoever gets to the highest number wins. (5 points)

♦ With a partner, take turns reading each other phone numbers until both of you have filled in the numbers missing on your sheet. Then compare sheets. (5 points)

Application Level

Choose two:

♦ Read a children's book on numbers (in target language) to at least three students at once. (10)

♦ Watch a video, and write down the numbers you hear the announcer say. (10)

♦ Tell the teacher your telephone number (with area code), locker combination, and student ID number, and also read a number drawn from the slips of paper in the jar. (10)

♦ Tell the teacher your birthday and that of a parent or guardian, including the year of birth. (10)

♦ Tell the teacher your phone number, a friend's number, and read one from a page in the phone book that you are given. (10)

Mastery Level

Choose one:

♦ Recite the numbers zero to 100 without errors. (15)

♦ Count to 100 by fives, forward and backward. (15)

♦ Take and pass (80 percent) a spelling quiz over numbers between zero and 100. (15)

Tiered Lesson: Sports (Tiered by Process)
Layered-Curriculum Type

Student assignments list: **Sports and Leisure Unit**　75 points possible
Basic rules:

♦ Your name must be on everything.

♦ Do at least one item per day. Classroom participation is part of your grade. Hand in this paper with your work so that the teacher may initial the proper space(s).

♦ Do not lose this paper, because it must be turned in at the end of the unit for your grade. If you lose it, you will need to start over and redo all assignments.

♦ All students will take the unit test, regardless of level chosen.

Final due date for this unit is: _____

Name: _____

C-level: Do 50 points from this section.

- Do all workbook activities for the chapter, checked, corrected, and stapled together. (20)

- Do the verb work sheet. (10)

- Read the chapter, and complete the graphic organizer. (10)

- Complete writing assignment #1. (10)

- Complete writing assignment #2. (10)

- Complete writing assignment #3. (10)

- Submit daily notes from class. (5)

- Do a word search. (5)

- Tell the teacher what your favorite sport is, where you do it, who you do it with, and how often. (5)

- Review the work sheet. (10 points)

B- level: Choose one or more, to earn at least 15 points.

- Write what you and your family did on your last vacation. Mention what each member did individually and what you all did together, as well as one thing you did not do. (15 points)

- Write a review of a sports event you attended recently. (15 points)

- Complete the listening activities in class (must get 80 percent correct for the teacher to sign off on this). (5 points each, up to two)

- Design a poster for your favorite sport. Show the equipment, and make a list of useful vocabulary in the target language. (5 points)

- With a partner or alone, make up a short (three-activity) exercise routine and lead the class in doing it. (5 points)

A-level: Choose one of these, for 10 points.

- With a partner, prepare a TV sports news broadcast or a sportscast (narrate a sports match) for the sport of your choice. Present it for the class. (10 points)

- Write a Little Book on sports. Each page must have at least one sentence and an illustration. You will be graded on correct spelling and grammar. (10 points)

- Make a scrapbook of a trip (real or imaginary) that you've taken during which you did sports and activities typical of the area you vacationed. It must include pictures or drawings (at least 10) and comments for each picture. (10 points)

Checklists for Differentiated Units

Use this checklist before and during a unit.

Checklist for a Differentiated Lesson or Unit

Unit: _____   Level: _____

Big Rocks: _____

_____

☐ I have determined what I want students to know (facts).

☐ I have determined what I want students to understand (principles, ideas).

☐ I have determined what I want students to be able to do at the end of this unit.

☐ In choosing Content, I've decided to differentiate (check at least one):

○ Sources/resources

○ Support for content: partners, tapes, direct instruction, organizers, and so on

○ Pacing for different ability levels

☐ I've decided how to preassess (or have already preassessed) student readiness.

☐ I've provided a variety of activities, for students with more than one learning style.

☐ In assigning students to groups and/or tasks, I've made sure:

○ That group assignments are flexible and change fairly often (or students may work alone if desired)

○ That students are encouraged to "work up" (try a level that challenges them)

☐ All the assignments (check at least one):

○ Vary along a continuum of Bloom's taxonomy or other measure of cognitive development

○ Call for higher-level thinking

○ Appear almost equally interesting to students

○ Give students choices about how to apply skills or how to express them

○ Accommodate a variety of learning styles or ability levels

☐ My lesson gives students choices of ways to demonstrate essential learnings.

☐ My lesson provides (check at least two):

○ Clear expectations for content (what skills must be demonstrated, what resources must be used) so that students understand the objectives of the unit

○ Clear expectations for process (goal setting, use of time, self-evaluation, etc.)

○ Clear expectations for high-quality product (rubric for criteria, clear method of assessment)

○ For self-assessment by student as well as by teacher

☐ Assessment is related to objectives and standards.

☐ Time allotment allows objectives to be accomplishable by all students.

☐ I have a means for bringing closure and clarity to the unit.

Checklist for Observing a Lesson or Unit That Uses Differentiated Instruction

☐ I can identify the unit of instruction being addressed.

☐ It is obvious that a diagnosis of student needs, learning styles, or interests has taken place.

☐ I see flexible grouping in this lesson or unit.

☐ I see evidence of "respectful tasks" for students (that is, the tasks neither bore students nor drive them too hard).

☐ There is evidence of ongoing monitoring and assessment of the success of the lesson.

☐ There is differentiation of (check at least one):

○ Content

○ Process

○ Product

☐ I see indications that the lesson or unit has been (or will be) adjusted according to student mastery of knowledge, understandings, or skills.

5

Ideas Smorgasbord

This is not a chapter for lesson plans but rather lots of ideas to use in planning. One of the keys to a differentiated classroom is to have many types of activities to choose from when setting up a differentiated lesson—a smorgasbord, where the students pick and choose what looks good to them.

Let's begin with a list of activities grouped according to how much time they will take you to plan and get ready to implement

Low-Prep Differentiated Activities	*High-Prep Differentiated Activities*
Brainstorming	Alternative assessments
Choice of homework	Compacting
Choice of journal prompts	Flexible grouping
Choice of readings	4MAT
Computer programs for practice or review	Graduated rubrics
Exploration by interests	Graphic organizer (plus lecture)
Games to practice mastery of info	Independent study
Grid assignments (tic-tac-toe menu)	Interest groups
Jigsaw	Learning or interest centers
Journal	Literature circles
Ladders	Mentorships
Mind mapping	Multiple tests
Mini-lessons to reteach	Multiple texts
Multiple levels of questions (i.e., Bloom's)	Problem-based learning
Open-ended activities	Send-a-Problem
RAFT assignment	Simulations
Reading buddies	Team games and tournaments
Self-evaluation checklists	Tiered activities
Student goal-setting	Total Physical Response Storytelling (TPRS)
Think-Pair-Share	
Working alone or with someone else	

Also, I'd like to point out that some of the above activities can be used only for more advanced groups. You may want to use the following list to help with planning (especially of tiered lessons).

Level 1		Level 2	Level 3+ (Advanced)
		All activities listed in Level 1, and:	All activities listed for Levels 1 and 2, and:
KWL and KWLH	Battleship	Group reading	Word web
Practice grid	Find Someone	Never!	Why?
Grid game	Who...	Trade-Off	Circumlocution
(vocabulary)	Survey	Telephone	Hot Seat
Chunking	Name it or	message	Botticelli
Rebus stories	Wear it	You Don't Say!	Elaboration
Visuals, props	Dialogicals	What's My Line	Word Splash
Manipulatives	Inside-Outside	Describe and	Opinion survey
Personalization	Circles	draw	Time Line
Flash cards	Ladders	Educated guess	Jigsaw (reading)
Everyday text	Simulations	Flowchart	Literature circle
Invitations	Stimulations	SQ3R	Poetry gallery
Gestures	Role play	Mind map	Double-entry
Music	I've Got It	Reader's Theater	journal
Telephone	Recitation	Scrapbook	Blogging
Ticket out	Venn diagram	Cornell note	Fairy tale
Line-ups	WebQuest	taking	Writing
Flip book	Roll 'n' Rock	RAFT	follow-ups
Little book	Creator	Password	
ABC book	Verb Turkeys		
Learning centers			

And now for the activities!

Vocabulary

There are three categories of vocabulary used in every classroom, and there are ways to differentiate its learning.

Vernacular

The first, vernacular vocabulary, consists of words that students may see only on a vocabulary list but never hear in a real context that would be of use to all students.

Choose a list of at least 25 words, preferably some the students will hear reinforced in other subject areas, post them in the classroom, and use them whenever possible. Encourage and reward students for using them, correctly and naturally, in speech and in writing. Make sure the list is realistic and practical.

Examples of some that would be on my list: perspective, pejorative, comportment, pilgrimage, colloquial.

How does this qualify as differentiated instruction, in light of the fact that all students get the same list?

♦ Students begin to use the words at their own pace.

♦ Students learn the words in various ways. They hear the teacher and their peers use them in context, they see them on the wall, they get social interaction when using them (encouragement, congratulations), and they write the words as well as say them.

♦ Advanced learners will begin to use them in expanded forms: variants, root words, related words, complex sentences.

Academic

The second category, academic vocabulary, is made up of words that are probably already in students' vocabulary, that are used frequently in academic language, but that students need to be encouraged to use effectively.

I encourage my students to use what I call transition words, beginning in level 1:

English	French	Spanish	German
first	d'abord	primero	zuerst
next	puis	próximo	nächste
then	alors	entonces	dann
finally	enfin, finalement	finalmente	schließlich
afterward	après, ensuite	después	danach
following, therefore, consequently	ensuite par conséquent	por consiguiente	deshalb, infolgedessen
but	mais	pero	aber
thus	donc	así	so

| nevertheless | *néanmoins* | *no obstante* | *trotzdem* |
| every time | *chaque fois, toutefois* | *cada vez* | *jedes Mal* |

In more advanced classes, we learn to use "argument words," such as the following:

English	*French*	*Spanish*	*German*
because	*parce que, à cause de, car*	*porque*	*weil*
except	*sauf, à part*	*excepto*	*außer*
although	*bien que*	*aunque*	*obwohl*
even if	*même si*	*cuando*	*auch wenn*
however	*cependant*	*sin embargo*	*aber*
according to	*selon*	*según*	*nach*

Classroom Vocabulary

The third, and most common, category is classroom vocabulary, which falls into two subsets. One is subject-specific *terminology*, which students will probably use only in your classroom. Words such as "stem," "root" (grammar), "conjugate," "determiner," "subjunctive," "preterit," or even "culture" or "stereotype" might fall into this category.

The second one that we all struggle with is the target language (TL) *unit vocabulary.*

Teaching the Vocabulary in a Unit

Does this sound familiar? On Monday, or several days a week, students are presented with 10 or more new words and definitions whose pronunciations and definitions are given. Students copy the words down and then use them to do workbook exercises, make flash cards, or write sentences, in class and as homework. Every Friday is a quiz covering the week's words. Good students do well, and weak students don't.

In a differentiated classroom, students begin to show an interest in words, use them in speech and writing, and remember them; no more class time is used this way than with the other method. There are quite a few ways to achieve these results.

Use Choice

In many chapters, there are a few nonnegotiable words, those that are essential and must be learned. For the rest of the vocabulary, you may have students choose only half the words to study, using the following criteria:

♦ Let students select words they have heard but have never used or aren't sure how to use.

♦ Let them select words that seem interesting or useful to them.

♦ Let them decide both how to practice and how to be assessed. Let them decide what their vocabulary quiz will be: Hand out a piece of paper with 10 lines on it. Let each student select which 10 words he or she will be quizzed on. Several days later, let each take the quiz on the chosen words; the teacher supplies either the definition or a sentence, depending on the teacher's teaching style, the students' learning level, the teacher's choice, or the students' choice (no matching allowed).

♦ Give students three different vocabulary lists: one easier, one of medium difficulty, and a harder one, with extra points awarded for those attempting the more difficult levels. Make sure the lists are not just divided up according to how many syllables they have. Put on the harder list those words that have different usages or connotations of that are subtler, no matter how easy they are to spell or say.

Grid Game

Another vocabulary game I learned from a colleague gives students a choice of which words are practiced as a group. First, give students a grid like that below.

Grid Game Blank

1	2	3	4	5	6
7	8	9	10	11	12

They put their initials or name in space 1, and a vocabulary word of their choice (or its English equivalent—you decide) in each space. Then, as a group, each with his or her own paper, they take turns rolling a pair of dice. If, for example, the student rolls a four, he or she does one of the following: uses the word in a sentence, translates it, or draws a picture of it. If the group approves what he or she does, the student puts his or her initials or name in the box and passes the dice to the next person. If that student throws the same number on the next turn, he or she gets to try the same thing on someone else's 4 space on their paper. If no 4s are left, he or she loses a turn. The game continues until every space has a name on it; the winner is whoever got his or her name in the most spaces. (This can also be used to have students conjugate verbs: put a verb in every space, and have the students write logical sentences in a given verb tense.)

Another way to afford choice is to use a vocabulary grid.

Unit: Family Vocabulary

The following table is an example of a practice grid I use to give students choices. They must select five to do for this unit. Sometimes I require that all five they select touch on the grid (which limits the students' choices but provides more variety in the types of activities they do).

Use five words, each in a Juicy Sentence (at least 10 words long): who, what, where, why, when, how.	Draw a family tree, labeling each member with their name and relationship to you (don't forget articles!).	Call my voice mail and leave me a message in which you use four words meaningfully to tell me about your family.
Make a word search using chapter vocabulary. Have someone do the word search and initial it.	Make a Memory Model mnemonic for four words that have no similarity to English.	Write a story using vocabulary from the chapter, and tape yourself reading it.
Make a rebus (picture story), using at least six vocabulary words, and have someone read it back to you.	Make a crossword, using as many chapter words as possible. Have a classmate do the crossword and initial it.	Invent a family, and make a family album, at least five pages long, with a sentence for each page. Pictures may be cut out or drawn.
With a partner, make a storyboard or cartoon about family members, with captions or dialogue for each cell.	Take a familiar tune and make a family song, using vocabulary from this unit, and sing it (or have someone sing it) to me.	Write a skit about a family, and perform it (or get someone to perform it) for the class.
Go on the Internet and read about the _____ royal family. Draw their family tree and label it, using chapter vocabulary.	Make up riddles about five words in the chapter, such as "My mother's brother's daughter is my _____."	Make a set of picture flash cards for chapter vocabulary.
Get four friends together and introduce yourselves to the class as a "family," with names, relationships, and one more detail each.	Write a poem about a family member. Mention how you and two other people are related to the person in the poem.	Put on a puppet show about a family who meets a stranger and discover he or she is a distant relative of theirs.

Use Context

Use the words yourself, frequently, and make the kids use them, in sentence form. Give rewards for word sightings: seeing a food vocabulary word on a label and bringing it to class, etc. Require students to write so-called *Juicy Sentences*—that is, longer ones that recycle old vocabulary and answer the who, what, where, when, and how questions. For example, instead of "Mary plays baseball," you get "Mary plays baseball after school at four o'clock with her friends."

A *vocabulary journal* is a great context-based method and a continuing anchor activity that students can always be working on when they finish early. You pick and choose from several different elements for a vocabulary journal—sort of like from a restaurant menu—according to what you'd like your students to be doing.

Give students, or teach them to draw, a page with columns on it, like a chart. The left-hand part is a column for the vocabulary word. You may provide students with the vocabulary word or have them select the words they wish to record. (Remember, I advocate giving students choices, but occasionally I mandate a "very important" word.)

Then, in other columns beside that word, have them do some or all of the following:

- Guess what the word means in English.

- Give context clues (e.g., noun markers, appositives, photos) that help make that guess.

- Draw a picture to go with the word.

- Define the word in English (you decide whether or not they may use a dictionary).

- Use the word in a sentence. (Slower students could just copy the sentence it was used in; average students could write an original sentence, and advanced students could write a Juicy Sentence.).

- Find a synonym for the word in the target language.

Use Chunking

Teach nine (the top number of items the brain can handle at once, according to brain research) or fewer key words and associated words. For example, on a family unit we learn "mother," "father," "sister," "brother," "grandmother," "grandfather," "aunt," "uncle," and "cousin" and two adjectives with each. My students choose the adjectives: a loving or strict mother, a fun or hardworking father, a silly or pretty sister, an annoying or tall brother, and so on. And we always use the same words together in the beginning. Then each set counts to the brain as only one item. As students get more familiar with the words, they mix and match the adjectives: a silly father, a pretty mother, and so on. This has another advantage for reading: Fluent readers don't read individual words; they read groups of words. Teaching students words in clumps encourages them to look and listen for word groups instead of individual words.

For sports, you can do the sport with the equipment and the body part used: "In tennis I hit the ball with a racquet," "In soccer, I hit the ball with my head," and so on. Teach professions with places to work, clothing with weather—there are endless possibilities.

Another type of chunking activity is a word web, a graphic organizer that resembles a web. For an example in English, see the following display.

Word Web

To make a word web, begin by writing a word in the middle of a blackboard, on an overhead transparency, or on paper. Enclose it in a circle, and then ask students to brainstorm related words. As they come up with the words, you write them, circle them, and attach them to the central circle with a line. As students come up with more words, the graphic will resemble a web. Words that are related go in the same circle.

Word webs are good for introducing new vocabulary, writing poetry (getting synonyms), or (in the case above) encouraging students to use more variety when writing.

Find Patterns

Compare/contrast is a great learning tool. When learning the names of common objects, think about whether they are new (recent inventions) versus old. For clothing, organize it according to whether it is worn by males, females, or either sex—and use that to examine gender. Why are some things men wear feminine, or vice versa? List the words for male professionals and female (*profesor, profesora/ Lehrer, Lehrerin/ infirmier, infirmière*), and use that list to discuss common gender endings. Another way to organize words is by positive or negative intensity: List answers to "How are you?" according to how good or bad students feel; this works well with emotions and descriptive adjectives, too. A third way is to encourage students to categorize the words: things to eat, drink, or ingredients.

Use Associations

Try to link the words, if possible, to English words they know, or other TL words (an example of both might be the French word *tapis,* or rug, which is related to *tapisserie,* tapestry). For the body parts *doigt, pied,* and *main* (finger, foot, and hand), I point out that things we use fingers for are *digital,* feet operate a *pedal,* or my car has a *manual* transmission. For the ones without easy associations, you may use Memory Model to manufacture associations unique to each person, group, or class. (Memory Model is explained in Chapter 3.)

Use Visuals

Post pictures of vocabulary, and have students draw pictures on their flash cards. Have kids write and read rebus stories, which use pictures in place of some words. Make mobiles with vocabulary words and visual representations of them, and hang them up. Have students make and show PowerPoint presentations.

Personalize

Ask questions about the students that use the vocabulary, have students interview each other about their real life (their bedrooms, sports, health habits, etc.) A PowerPoint presentation using photos of students in the class is a great way to practice clothing, emotions, descriptive adjectives, and so on.

Tell Stories

Total Physical Response Storytelling (TPRS) does this well, or read a children's book with the vocabulary in it. Have students participate in information-gap activities, in which they talk to each other using partner sheets—papers on which each student has only half the information needed to complete the paper.

Use Manipulatives

We all undoubtedly teach time by giving students a clock with movable hands. Carry over this kinesthetic learning style to other chapters. The easiest way is to write them on separate cards and then have students sort words into categories that either you or they devise. For example, in an adjective chapter, there are many categories to use. For adjectives, positive, negative, or neutral; beauty, age, goodness, or size; synonym and antonym (my favorite, because if they can't remember the right word, they can always say the opposite—e.g., instead of "short," they can say "not tall"); or looks, personality, size, or miscellaneous. They can also fill in graphic organizers. For a food chapter, have the students draw a meal on a paper plate and practice ordering what's on different plates, or they can call out a food and have everyone with that item on their plate raise their plate. In the clothing unit, use real clothes or paper dolls. Have students write vocabulary words and their definitions (or pictures) on opposite sides of a line on a puzzle sheet, cut them apart, stir up the pieces, and then put the puzzle back together.

Read, Read, Read

The speed at which students learn new words is directly proportional to their exposure to them. But this doesn't mean fill-in-the-blanks or matching. The words need to be in sentences, in paragraphs. The more times students run across a word in context, the better. Send them to Internet sites to shop for furniture, give them restaurant menus to order food, read children's books to them or with them, read plays and novels—anything they would enjoy and be interested in. My soccer players who turned up their noses at stories in the book read everything in the soccer magazines I brought back with me from overseas—even the ads.

Use Gestures

Studies done on people with brain injuries after a serious accident have found that words may often be retrieved when they are associated with a gesture, because they were stored in two areas of the brain instead of just one. Making the gesture of writing recalled the word "pen"—and try saying "castanets" without making the clicking motion! I like to practice verbs especially by associating gestures with them (a good TPRS technique), and I often see my students making gestures during a test. If they ask me how to say a verb they already know, all I have to do is make the gesture to remind them of it.

Use Music

Authentic music is good, but so is putting vocabulary or grammar to a familiar tune. We sing the days of the week to the theme of "The Flintstones," and my students still complain that every time they hear the tune of "Jingle Bells," they have to sing the possessive adjectives instead of the English.

♦ *Mon, ma, mes*

♦ *Ton, ta, tes*

♦ *Son, sa ses, la la!*

♦ *Notre, nos,*

♦ *Votre, vos*

♦ *Leur et leurs, voilà!*

Of course, I'm thrilled that they can't forget the French.

To summarize, teachers need a wide array of activities and exercises involving conversational contexts and reinforcements. Learning must be contextual and enthusiastic if it is to be lasting. Students need to read and listen, guess from context, and elaborate to really learn new vocabulary.

Speaking, Listening

Some of the following activities are differentiated in nature automatically. Others, though not differentiated activities themselves, might be good to include as choices for a differentiated lesson, as part of a practice grid like the one in the previous section on vocabulary, or in a tiered lesson as one of the choices in a tier section.

Telephone

This is not the old party game (although that would be good, too) but, rather, a game to encourage good listening and correct pronunciation. As with the game, you begin by lining up the students (the longer the line, the more difficult it will be, so it's best to use short lines for lower levels). At one end of the line are objects, flash cards, or pictures that suggest vocabulary (nouns, verbs, adjectives, even interrogative pronouns). One student (or the teacher) whispers a word, phrase, or sentence in the ear of the person at the end of the line farthest from the pictures or objects. At your cue, the person then whispers it to the next person and so on down the line, eventually to the person at the end closest to the flash card or object, and that person physically picks up the flash card or object and shows it. The last person goes to the other end of the line so everyone gets a chance.

Variations: For this variation, with easier prep, there's no picture or object at the end, just chalk, and the last student writes the whispered bit of language on the board. A fun variation: At the end of the line is clothing, and the person must put on an outfit whispered to him or her—or take off an item, if he or she dressed in clothing before the activity began. In another variation, a command is whispered, and the last person does whatever the command was: pick up a pencil, hit the chair, and so on. Still another variation is for the last person to have to take a bite of whatever food was whispered.

Ticket Out

This is my favorite form of speaking as well as a great assessment: to get out of class at the end of the period, students must say something, usually related to the main point of the day's lesson or something they'll be required to say at the end of the unit (or for whatever high-stakes test they give in your state).

Line-Ups

Students are asked to line up according to height, birth-day, middle initial, their opinion on a given topic, their favorite color (lining up on the ROY G BIV color spectrum), shoe size, how many brothers they have, or whatever the unit is on. This goes quickly and is easy to check, and you can easily bend the line at the middle and give everyone a partner for the next activity.

Never!

Great for verb-conjugation practice, Never! can be played in any tense. As preparation, have students be ready to tell three to five things they never do now, have never done (past tense), will or would never do. (Warning from my own experience—tell them they can't use anything involving a bodily function, or you'll get boys talking about tampons and worse things.) Then form a circle, and give everyone some sort of marker—a dried lima bean, a coin, or something that will make a loud plunk when dropped into the container—and pass a container around; take turns starting the container. The first person with the container says a "never" statement, and people who *have* done this thing put in a marker. The object is to be either the first one to run out of markers or the last.

Why?

Have a student volunteer to be in the hot seat and make a statement. The class then asks in chorus, "Why?" and the student volunteer must say something in the target language that makes sense. Give one point for every successful response. See who can get the highest score in the class or group. (Yes, this does work in smaller groups; each small group can have its own hot seat.) My students really enjoy this, and it helps get them to speak longer and more fluently (and trains them for Juicy Sentences—see the section on writing).

Trade-Off!

Students in groups of two, each with a blank paper and writing instrument, flip a coin to see who goes first. I announce a topic, set my kitchen timer for a given time, and tell them to begin. The first student begins speaking and must speak continuously on the topic, though he or she is allowed to ask the partner (in the target language) for help with a word. Student B writes down everything student A says. When the timer rings, they trade roles (make sure student A turns the paper over, or some may just read what's there). When the timer rings again, have them exchange papers and correct any errors in what was written (or assign them to bring in a clean copy the next day).

Battleship

This is played exactly like the board game, but on a piece of paper. See page 111 for an example of a Battleship grid for French. Students fill in four "ships" in blanks in a grid their partner cannot see. Then they take turns guessing the various spaces by saying (or writing) the correct answer for the space they wish to guess. For example, in the display on page 111, if one wanted to guess the top left space, one would say "je rougis." If what was said is correct, the partner replies with whether that space was a hit (part of a ship there), a miss, (nothing there), or a "sunk" (the final portion of a ship to be hit). If they have a hit, they may continue guessing; a miss response ends the turn, and someone else takes over. The winner is the first to sink all the partner's ships.

Battleship

Review these present-tense verbs. Mark the following in the grid (no diagonals)

   one ship of two spaces = *un croiseur* (cruiser)

   two ships of three spaces = *un destroyer*

   one ship of four spaces = *un porte-avions* (aircraft carrier)

   Vocabulary: *manqué* ("missed"), *frappé* ("hit"), *coulé* ("sunk"), *dommage,* ("too bad"), *nananere* = ("ha-ha!"—mocking), *zut!* ("darn!"), *tricheur!* ("cheater")

	je	*tu*	*il/elle*	*nous*	*vous*	*ils/elles*	English meaning
rougir							
finir							
entendre							
écouter							
choisir							
grossir							
perdre							
détester							
répondre							
vendre							

Variations: Battleship may also be played with nouns and adjectives (making the adjective match in gender and number) or with pictures (students say a sentence with words about both pictures to guess that space). You can also give students blank grids and have them fill the edges with words they discuss and choose from a list (more talking to negotiate what vocabulary or verbs will be used). If you use this as an independent activity, I'd advise you to have the students write their guesses on paper so you can either swing by to correct errors or collect it as evidence that they actually did play the game (and correct errors later, if you were working with a different group.)

Telephone Message

I am fortunate to have a telephone in my room with a system whereby people can leave messages for me. So, for almost every unit we do, I require students to call me and leave a message. They must do the following: greet me, state their name, perform the required task (see examples that follow) and say good-bye.

At various times my students will call and tell me their favorite activity and ask me what mine is, invite me to do something with them, and tell where and when it will be; spread untrue gossip about a classmate whose name they have drawn (the wilder the better; really high interest is generated when we listen to the messages, and students get quite creative); describe their favorite meal, music, family member and tell why it's their favorite; list three things they must do to be healthy and give me a suggestion on something I should do as well—the possibilities are endless.

I usually give several days for the students to call and then we play the messages back. I give them a graphic of some sort to fill out as they listen (food categories to write favorites and who they belong to, for example) or assign them, in the gossip case, to listen for their own name and tell the class that no, they did not do whatever it was, or they are horrified, or some sort of reaction we've practiced prior to listening.

Survey

This one is just like it sounds. Give students a grid to fill out such as this one:

Student's name	Favorite room in house and why	Color of room	Floor it's on	Furniture in room

Of course, they ask and answer questions and fill in the grid, using the target language.

Find Someone Who...

This is a standard technique in most teachers' bag of tricks, and often included in communicative-activity packets provided by publishers. In this activity, a student survey such as the one in the grid above can be collected and used by the teacher to prepare a list of students to be found.

Find someone who:

◆ Has a blue bedroom

◆ Watches TV in the basement

◆ Likes his or her kitchen best of all

◆ Has a waterbed

◆ Has a desk in his or her room

It's okay if statements fit more than one student. My lists, such as the one above, would be in French rather than English, and students must change the verb from third person to second person when interviewing classmates.

You can give students a limited amount of time to find someone for each statement and have them initial their own spot, or it can be an anchor activity that they do whenever they find time during the unit, and turn in before the final assessment takes place.

You Don't Say!

This is adapted from the popular game Taboo. In this, students are given a word or phrase and several associated forbidden words, and must talk about the target word without using any of the forbidden words. For example, the word might be "cake," and they cannot say "chocolate," "dessert," or "sweet."

Name It or Wear It

This might just be my students' favorite game, but we do it at most once a year. I have, over the years, collected some spectacularly ugly, outsized, or tiny, outlandish clothing (yellow, red, and black cowboy boots, a Star Trek jersey, a plaid plastic raincoat, a baby-size cheerleader costume, etc.), which I store in laundry baskets. When we do a unit on colors, clothing, shopping, demonstrative pronouns, or advanced-level description that includes fabric types, I get out the clothing and, choosing a student randomly, reach into the basket, pull out an item, and ask him or her to describe its color(s) or tell what it is or tell which one they'd prefer. If they can't, they must take the item and, when the basket is empty, wear whatever they have collected. At my students' request, I allow people who have successfully described an article to choose a classmate who must wear it. Then out comes the digital camera, and we immortalize the students in their new outfits; then, to be allowed to remove the garments, the unfortunate wearers must describe them to a chosen partner. The students are highly motivated to correctly identify the items, and the next day when the pictures come out, the clothing can be used for oral descriptions or a written exercise (review or assessment): "Bill is wearing a pink feather boa and very large purple paisley shorts with fuzzy gold slippers…"

Props

 Give students something to hold and talk about. A poster, a stuffed animal (tell its name and life story, or five things it likes, or what it did yesterday or will do tonight), a suitcase of objects that suggest a sport or a city or region in a TL country, a work of art depicting a family to make up a story about—students always seem to talk more and enjoy talking more when they have something to look at or hold.

Dialogicals

In a form such as that below, you write half a dialogue. The paper is then split down the middle, and each half is given to one student in a paired discussion. Student A reads his or her sentence, and student B writes down what was said; then student B reads his or hers and A writes the response. Together they decide whether the resulting conversation is logical or illogical. This activity is good for pronunciation and listening skills.

Dialogicals

1. A) _____   1. A) _____
    B) _____   B) _____

2. A) _____   2. A) _____
    B) _____   B) _____

3. A) _____   3. A) _____
    B) _____   B) _____

4. A) _____   4. A) _____
    B) _____   B) _____

5. A) _____   5. A) _____
    B) _____   B) _____

The following display is a filled-out example in Spanish.

Spanish Dialogicals (Example)

1. A) ¿Cómo te llamas?

    B) _____

2. A) ¿Cuál es la fecha?

    B) _____

3. A) ¿Qué hora es?

    B) _____

4. A) ¿Cómo estás?

    B) _____

5. A) ¿Cuál es el tiempo?

    B) _____

6. A) ¿Cómo se dice "I'm hungry"?

    B) _____

7. A) Me gustaría algunos dulces.

    B) _____

8. A) ¿Cuántos años tienes?

    B) _____

9. A) ¿Tienes hambre?

    B) _____

10. A) ¿Qué hora es?

    B) _____

1. A) _____

    B) Soy de Madrid.

2. A) _____

    B) Es el diez de marzo.

3. A) _____

    B) Es lunes

4. A) _____

    B) Muy bien, y tu?

5. A) _____

    B) Llueve

6. A) _____

    B) Tengo sed.

7. A) _____

    B) Yo también

8. A) _____

    B) Tengo dieciséis años

9. A) _____

    B) Un poco

10. A) _____

    B) Es cansado

Circumlocution

In Circumlocution, students are given a word, phrase, or idea that either doesn't exist in the target culture (e.g., Jell-O, hayride, cheerleader) and are asked to describe it in the target language until a partner can guess it, or are given a TL word (this works well with things like clothing, furniture, hygiene supplies, such as hairbrush and lipstick) and must again describe it until the partner guesses the word: "You use it in the morning to clean your teeth. It is long and thin." This is a great skill to have in real life, as many times students might forget the precise word and need to use circumlocution to communicate.

Inside-Outside Circles

Also called Dyadic, this game involves two groups of students facing each other in pairs in a circle. This formation facilitates discussion with a variety of partners. There are many ways to implement this situation; I use it often for question-and-answer series in the text or to practice certain phrases. One student asks a question, and the partner answers; then one or both circles rotate so students have new partners, and they repeat the process. Often I will provide the "answer" student with a specific word or phrase he or she must use in the answer. This is also a good way for students to present skits, because they must perform the skit multiple times and have time to get feedback from their listeners; also, doing the skit in front of a small group instead of a full class can really help somewhat insecure or shy students feel better about being successful in speaking.

Simulation

Simulations are the meat of world-language teaching. We try to make things as real as possible for our students, and try to create the same real-life conditions in the classroom that students will encounter in a foreign country. Entire books have been written on simulations (teaching native dances, eating habits, etc.). Speaking simulations in the classroom would require students to have a "passport" and go through customs to enter the classroom, check into the "hotel" (classroom again), buy an item lying on the desk as they enter or leave, and so on. The more of these you can do, the better: Assign students to write and lead an exercise routine.

Stimulations

This is a collection of items that encourages students to talk. One is a bowl of M&M's. I tell students to take a handful but not to eat them. In level 1, when we learn colors, we use M&M's to talk about how many of each color we have, and we name the colors as we eat the candy. Later, I hand out the M&M's, but this time for each M&M, the students must say one sentence, using vocabulary and a specific grammar point. In later levels, with the same strategy, students who want to get out of speaking will take just one or two M&M's; for those classes, I tell the students that they must subtract a number from what they've taken and that all resulting negative numbers become positive, and they owe me that many; for example, the number might be 14, and if they only took two M&M's, they owe me 12. People who took a more reasonable number owe me very few sentences…

A similar strategy involves the use of a roll of toilet paper. Students are asked to take a length of TP, and do something like list their favorite things, tearing off a square of TP for each thing they mention, and throwing it on the floor or over their shoulder. They really enjoy doing both: taking the paper and throwing it.

A third stimulator is a jar of bubble fluid and a bubble wand. Students take turns waving the wand to make bubbles, and then they must talk about a topic (a good one is themselves as a getting-to-know-you activity early in a level 2 or 3 class) until every bubble has burst. This activity is very popular with kids of every age.

A final technique that I first did as a mixer at a club meeting, involves a ball of yarn. Hand the ball to a student volunteer and ask him or her to say something about him- or herself, and any students who feel that that statement is also true for themselves ask for the ball. The first student holds on to the end of the ball and throws it to another. The second student makes a different statement, holds on to the yarn, and throws it to another, and so on until everyone has had the yarn at least once. The students see others in the classroom with whom they have something in common; also, you will learn more about your students, and you can talk about connections between people, and between languages, one of the national standards.

Role Play

 A role play is a bit different from a simulation, in that students are asked to be someone other than their real selves. For example, the students who play the waiter in a café skit are role players, whereas the students ordering are in a simulation. I've had lots of luck motivating my students to speak by creating a murder mystery, an action adventure à la Indiana Jones, and a soap opera for my advanced students. In these, students invent a (false) persona and stay in character to find a note, a clue, a dead body (in a murder mystery); spread gossip, write love letters, ask for advice, go to a hospital (in a soap opera); accuse someone of something and have a trial (a murder mystery or a soap); or get a mysterious telegram, explore a new region, find something with special powers, have their lives threatened and find a treasure (action-adventure story). Other teachers I've met, online or in the flesh, use other forms of role play: putting Goldilocks on trial for breaking and entering of the three bears' home; creating group "families" and letting students choose their names and relationships to the others, as well as a personal history; having students be interviewed by the class as they play the role of a famous person such as Columbus, Charlemagne, or Arnold Schwarzenegger. There was a cute suggestion that involved half the students in the class playing adults (with ties and other grown-up props) so students could practice the use of the proper form of "you" (*tu/vous, tu/usted, du/Sie,* or one of the many forms in Japanese). Some teachers group students with similar interests—fantasy, spies, horror, detective, superhero, Western, humor, and so on—and give them roles: a game master who creates the beginning scenario as well as some nonplayer characters that the other characters (students) have to deal with, and then the students create their own game. Some teachers even buy role-playing games—like Dungeons & Dragons, Ghostbusters, Gangbusters, or any of the hundreds of other games out there—but have students play them in the target language. You can also purchase CD-ROM games like Oscar Lake and others. Even shy students sometimes get braver when their characters, instead of their real selves, do and say things.

Question-and-Answer Activities

Here I've put together several Q & A activities I like to use: Hot Seat, What's My Line, Botticelli, and Elaboration.

Hot Seat

 I created this game many years ago based on my own experience talking to students in a French classroom. They fired questions at me, on any topic they wanted, as I did my best to understand what they were asking and to respond. In Hot Seat, I have students write 15 questions for their classmates. The questions may not be either-or or yes-and-no questions, and they also cannot be about anything obvious such as hair color or how many fingers someone has. Then, at intervals of my choosing over the next few weeks, one student takes his or her place in the hot seat (a special chair in my room) and answers 10 questions posed by classmates (everyone speaks in the target language). I don't make them answer in sentence form, because it's more realistic not to. (They do learn, however, that echoing the question is a good way to stall for time, and they also learn various ways to say "Ummm…") When students are not in the seat, they are required to ask 10 questions, one question of each of 10 classmates. I take notes as we do this activity and, at the end, give the class feedback on their participation and level of communication (or lack of it) as well as pronunciation errors.

What's My Line

This activity is a great way to practice asking questions as well. In this game, knowledge of a famous person is required, so it's best done after a unit on famous speakers of Spanish, French, German, Japanese, or another language. In What's My Line, the class asks questions of a student who plays the role of a famous person he or she has researched and knows well. Questions should be phrased so the answer is yes or no, and the answers help students guess who the famous person is. I usually limit the questions to 20.

Botticelli

This game is only for upper-level classes, because it's a much more complex version of What's My Line. With this activity, person A takes on the identity of a famous person and also supplies the first letter of the character's last name. But before students can ask a yes-or-no question of person A they must ask another question, on any topic they choose, that person A cannot answer or answers incorrectly. Example: "Who won the 2006 Super Bowl?" Answer: "The Chicago Cubs." Wrong answer, so the students may now ask a question about person A's identity: "Are you dead in 2005?" Whoever guesses the *it* person's identity first is next.

Elaboration

This game begins when one student says a subject and a (conjugated) verb. Each student afterward must add a word or phrase that continues the sentence, until someone cannot think of anything else to add. I have played Elaboration in a whole-class format (with a smaller, advanced class) and kept track of how many turns long the final sentence was, and then challenged the class to beat its own record for a reward, such as going to lunch two minutes early (or whatever motivates them). I've done it as a competition between two or more groups; the groups take turns adding to the sentence, and the ones who were last to add to the sentence get a point. I have had students do this with a partner and tell me who won. It's not only a great filler if you've got a few minutes left at the end of class; once they've learned the rules, it's a great way for the class to show off for a visiting administrator.

I've Got It!

To do this activity, the teacher must carefully prepare classroom sets of cards. I use 3 × 5 index cards divided in half. On the top half is one cue to listen for, and on the bottom is a speaking cue. These may be in English, in the target language, or in photos or illustrations copied from the text. One person starts (it doesn't matter who) by using the cue on the bottom half of the card. I often use these when we study the verb "to go": The first person, using his or her card, might say, "I am going to school." A second student, with school at the top of his or her card, would say, "I am going to school, too, and then I am going to [second cue, at the bottom half of card] the beach." Whatever student has that cue says, "I am going to the beach also, and then I am going to [another place]." and so on until the statements come back full circle to the person who began the series. This can be done as a timed activity; the class or group with the best time is rewarded. This activity works well with almost any category; students can talk about things to eat or wear, things they did yesterday (to practice past tense), pets they have, and many other subjects.

A more difficult variation is to have the top cue be not exactly what the person before them has said. To take the example of "to go" again: If the bottom cue used by the first student was "going to school," the top cue for the next student could be a logical thing to do there: "I'm going to study," the beach + to swim, the museum + to look at statues, and so on. This would have the benefit of using "to go" as a simple verb, and also as part of a present progressive verb.

Recitation

As a student, I was always happy to speak a bit of poetry or declaim a bit of Shakespeare for relatives, parents' friends, or anyone who said to me: "You're studying Spanish/French/Latin/German? Say something!" Now, as a teacher, I have all students memorize a short poem or nursery rhyme each semester and recite it for me. We also have verb songs, and memorize the lyrics, as well as the lyrics to popular songs in the target language. (It is said that when singing, everyone loses their American accent. We go Christmas caroling in French, too.) And so my students, many years later, will come up to me in a store or restaurant and recite part of something they learned in my class.

Describe and Draw

In this partner activity, student A has a picture (a photo, an illustration from the text, or even a famous painting by Picasso, Botero, or another artist.) He or she cannot show it to student B. Student A describes the picture, and student B draws it. The "artist" (student B) also will ask questions: big or small, higher or lower, etc. This activity also works with groups of three, especially if students are struggling or slow learners. The two students drawing can look at each other's picture for reinforcement and achieve more success than they would singly. When done, have them compare their artwork with the original, and then, if there's time, trade roles with a new picture.

Another version is to give students a drawing of a bowl and tell them to make a fruit salad. They should take turns suggesting an ingredient, and if the partner agrees to put it in the salad, the student draws that fruit in the bowl. If not, the student draws it outside the bowl. Then both will tell me (or another pair of students), using their drawing as a guide, what they will and will not put in the salad. This also works with toppings for a pizza, ingredients for a sub sandwich, furniture in a bedroom (or a dream house), body parts for a monster they create, and many other situations. It is important for the students to "read" their drawing back to someone. The teacher can also collect the drawings and have other groups try to read the drawing the next day as review.

Give One, Take One

For this activity, you can use the same 12-square grid as for the Grid Game (page 103) in the section on vocabulary. Have students reread the vocabulary words or expressions from the unit, and select three to write in the first three boxes of the grid. Then students roam to chosen partners; the pairs take turns reading their three chosen words to each other. Each time, a student selects a word or an expression from the other's list that is *not* on his or her own list and writes it in the next available empty box on the grid, saying in the target language: "I'll take _____." The partner does the same, and then each finds a different partner. This time, the new partners have four words to read, and choose a fifth to write down. If they have the same four, they say good-bye and find someone else. The students are *not* allowed to show their paper to the other student to read. When the grid is filled, this could easily become a writing activity; the students have to make a certain number of sentences, each of which uses one of the chosen words. Then the exercise could transform into a group speaking activity: Students could, for example, be grouped in five and read their sentences aloud; each group gets a point for every sentence no one else in the group has (similar to Scattergories). Or do it as a class, with groups taking turns to present a selected sentence and gaining a point if no other group had that sentence. Either way encourages creativity in writing the sentences.

Reading

There are quite a few strategies to use for reading, few of them very new, but here is an overview of all, offered up as choices for differentiating activities when reading.

Prereading

Wondering how to hook the students into reading? You could have students do a KWL (Know, Want to know, and Learned) sheet on the topic of the reading, or one of the other strategies listed here.

Word Splash

Tell students the subject of the reading, and have them brainstorm words they would expect to find in the reading, in the target language first and then in English (and you teach them the TL equivalent right then and there). Use a webbing strategy on the board, grouping vocabulary that is related (splash them across the board), and then ask students to see how many of these words are actually in the reading.

This can also be done as a group activity, with the students looking up in the dictionary any words they want to know and don't know yet and making their own Word Splash and then highlighting words they thought of and actually found, plus adding new words from the reading.

Have You Ever...

I often do an activity involving a survey of students' experiences or opinions. For example, before reading a story about a boy who wants a hockey shirt ("Le Chandail de Hockey"), I might give them this:

When I was younger, I really wanted something for my birthday.	Yes	No
Did you get it?	Yes	No
Was it as good as you thought it'd be?	Yes	No
I am a fan of a particular sports team.	Yes	No
I own clothing with a team's logo on it.	Yes	No
I have played or watched hockey.	Yes	No

After a quick show of hands, students are thinking about the basic ideas and topics in the story, and we are ready to read it with more understanding of what's going on than before the quick survey, and as a side benefit, I have learned a bit more about my students. (Keep the surveys short; you don't want to spend too much time on them.)

Reading Activities

Educated Guess

Encourage students to guess! Looking up every word will tire and frustrate them. Sometimes students will just look at a passage and say, "I can't do this." Making an educated guess is a way to make the task less daunting.

Step 1: Have students take just part of a passage you or they choose. Look at the pictures and headings, if any, and then have them highlight or cross out all *familiar* words and then look at what's left. Usually, the words they know greatly outnumber the others, and that relaxes them.

Step 2: Ask them to reread (or rewrite) the passage without the unknown words, and see if the simplified version still makes sense. If so, they can just forget those words for now, and keep reading.

Step 3: Is the word repeated several times in the next few sections? If it seems important, or they are very curious, have them make an educated guess on what it means (and have them write it down so they can refer to it later).

Step 4: Have them think of similar-looking or -sounding words in English, in hopes there might be a cognate. If that fails or has no definitive result, they should then look it up in the dictionary. Then they add it to a list of looked-up words they keep in their folder, and later I'll have them choose a certain number of those for a vocabulary quiz.

Graphic Organizers

Reading and graphic organizers are a match made in heaven. These are some graphic organizers I use frequently:

- ◆ Venn diagram
- ◆ Time line (or flowchart)
- ◆ SQ3R
- ◆ Mind map (also called concept map, with one variety known as clustering)

Venn Diagram

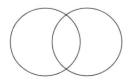

This is perhaps the most-used organizer. It usually consists of two large interlocking circles (it could also be stars, squares—any overlapping shape). Students using a Venn are encouraged to look for similarities and differences between two things as they read, and to write them in the diagram. I often use Venn diagrams to have students make contrasts between their own country and another country, for example, with a reading involving a school situation, a meal, or Christmas or another holiday. In the left circle, they write the customs, vocabulary, and so on, of the country they are reading about (which is different from their own). In the center overlap go those characteristics they read about that are similar. After the reading, the students review what they have written, and add customs of their own culture that are not on the diagram in the right circle. This can easily lead to a compare-or-contrast paper or discussion, facilitated by the Venn organizer; they can do these easily, with little or no help, because the organizer contains the vocabulary and ideas, already categorized. You can also walk around and see what they have written, gently suggesting or correcting as they work, or collect these for review overnight.

Flowchart

A flowchart, as it sounds, helps students reading a narrative to follow the flow of events. In the top box goes the original setting of the reading: who, what, when, and where. As events occur, each one goes below (in the chart pictured, the flowchart can flow both horizontally and vertically), accompanied vertically by additional information about the event (new characters, time period if it's a flashback, etc.)

Time Line

A time line is actually the same as a flowchart, but with a different look. It is simply a line drawn horizontally on the paper, sometimes with boxes or bubbles attached and ready to fill in, where students write down events from the reading in chronological order. Most of us have seen these in history texts, accompanied by text and pictures; there is no reason language students can't use pictures as well as words, because images aid storage of information in long-term memory and appeal to any learning style. This type of strategy will work for any narrative, however, and is really helpful when the students are reading a story with memories or flashbacks in it (such as *The Little Prince/Le Petit Prince/El Principito/Der kleine Prinz.*)

Here is a different way we use a time line when reading a biographical story: First, we set up the time line, using the person's age rather than dates, when the story is set during a long-ago time period. Our time line goes from birth to age 21. Using different colors, students list events from the reading in one color and write their own life stories in a different color. As they do this, they are struck by similarities and differences in the life of the main character (Joan of Arc or Rimbaud, for example), compared with their own lives.

SQ3R

This method, which has been around a long time, is useful for reading long passages. It has a well-proven track record as a useful reading tool.

"S" stands for Survey, and in this step the student looks at the title, illustrations, big headings, and writes them down—and makes a guess about the general topic of the work. This helps inform the students about the subject matter before they begin and puts it into context, which makes it more understandable.

"Q" stands for Questions, and every student, looking at the S section, writes down at least one question about what they have written in each of the who, what, where, and when sections. This serves the purpose of hooking the students into at least a mild interest in the selection to see if their guesses come true, as well as giving them things to look for when they're reading.

Then there are three Rs. The first "R" stands for Read, and as they read, the students answer their own questions. This is the only section they fill out while actually reading the selection. After finishing the selection, they do the two other Rs.

The second "R" is Recite, and, after reading the selection and completing the Read section, the students review both and list key words or ideas found in their answers or in the selection.

The third "R" is Review; here students summarize what the reading is about. As you can see from the form I use (page 127), I also ask them to react to the reading. Often in differentiated instruction, I ask for judgments or feedback as I let students select the readings, and if one is too difficult or is very unpopular, I'll try to find another.

SQ3R Form

S Title:

    Pictures of:

        Headings/subtitles:

    Guess:

        Who

        What

        Where

        When

Questions:

        1.

        2.

        3.

        4.

        5.

R

        1.

        2.

        3.

        4.

        5.

R   Important words and phrases:

Review:

    Summary of at least five sentences in length.

    Did you like this? Why or why not?

Mind Map

A mind map—also called a concept map (one variety is called clustering)—is a strategy created in the 1960s by Tony Buzan. With a mind map, students use a graphic organizer format full of colors and images to record words and ideas. Mind maps work well because they are adapted to the way the brain works, which is moving from thought to thought via associations, in a nonlinear form. If you've ever read stream-of-consciousness writing, you know what I mean. Any idea probably has thousands of links in long-term memory. Mind maps help students record, organize, and reinforce those associations and links, using just key words and key images, so they can get a lot of information on just one page.

How to Mind Map

- Start from the center of a page of plain paper (no lined paper). This gives room to go in any and every direction, even three-dimensionally.

- In the center, put a clear and strong visual image that depicts the general theme of the map.

- Put ideas down as they occur, wherever they fit. Don't pause, judge, or edit.

- Print, rather than write in script. Printing is more memorable *and* easier to read.

- Use just key words and, whenever possible, images. Anything that stands out on the page will stand out in the memory. Making students come up with an image to go with the words (creativity aids memory!) may be difficult, but it pays off.

- Use color, too, to reinforce various themes or associations and to make things stand out.

- Create subcenters for subthemes. If students see several ideas that are related, have them draw a circle around them or enclose them as a unit and draw an image to go with them.

- Don't get stuck in one area. If ideas dry up for one area, go to another branch.

- Use arrows, icons, or other visual aids to show links between different elements.

- Never start a new sheet if there's no more space: Tape or paste more paper onto the map where it's needed.

Things You Should See in a Good Mind Map

- *Branches.* A good mind map looks like a tree, a nerve system, a spider, a flower, a Fourth of July fireworks display—something with a center picture and things sprouting from it.

- *Lists and groupings.* Once students discover a subset for the main idea, they'll jot down all the words they can find for that subset before going on, enclosing it, and drawing an illustration.

- *Images.* Again, you may have to force this; I find my better students are used to just writing words. Coming up with an image for each subset makes them think more about its qualities and characteristics, and it's more memorable for everyone. And fun.

- *Arrows.* In the course of mapping, students often find one or more areas are related, and they indicate this by the use of arrows.

- *Explanatory sentences and notes.* It's not a bad idea to have students write a few comments on their map: explanations, questions, comments, or a summary.

Steps to Create a Mind Map

There are five steps suggested to create a mind map. They are similar to procedures for strategies found earlier in this chapter.

1. **Skim.** First read the introduction, conclusion, and headings and look at the illustrations (diagrams, pictures, or graphs). This gives an overview of the reading as well as its context and clues to where the most important information is located.

2. **Read.** If it's short, read it all at once, and then go back over any parts you're not sure of. If it's a whole book, break it apart into sections, or read just a chapter at a time.

3. **Mind map.** Now put away the reading and do the mind map from memory.

4. **Study.** Doing the mind map shows immediately what was learned well and where there are gaps in knowledge. First, try to pull up the information from memory. If that fails—and so does imagining what it might be—refer to the reading to fill in the gaps.

5. **Personalize.** Now add images, different colors, arrows, comments, and questions. Questions might be about relationships or clarity: How do the parts fit together? Does it all make sense? Is anything

missing or unclear? Is it all true? Useful? Comments might be about personal experience, implications for future events, or what was new to the mapper. What more would you need to know about this? Personalizing the mind map gives the student a review of the material and really helps enhance learning.

Then go looking for answers to any questions, or put the map away to review at a later date. Review daily if possible.

Uses of Mind Maps

+ Summarizing readings.

+ Summarizing lectures. Making a mind map is a good way to review or rewrite lecture notes.

+ Taking notes: meetings, interviews, phone conversations, or during a seminar or a workshop. Because notes from a mind map are non-linear and the student can jump from topic to topic and then return to them, this method is really useful for keeping track of what was said and for organizing and commenting on it.

+ Reviewing for an exam. Doing a mind map of the course content can point out the most important concepts and principles and the ways they fit together. This may also help a student discover weak areas and focus on studying those.

+ Solving problems. Mind maps help students see all the issues and their relationships, as well as their relative importance.

+ Speaking. Using a mind map as notes or memorizing it helps a student give a well-organized and coherent presentation. The visual nature of a mind map makes it easy to remember, as in "I pictured it in my head." Using the basic images of the mind map on an overhead or as a handout may help the audience as well.

+ Brainstorming. Mind maps are great for brainstorming whenever you want creativity. Tell students to just think of every item in a mind map as the center of another mind map and expand the map items until they find something that sounds good.

+ Research. After exploring and reading material on the writing topic, it's helpful to use a mind map to get all the relevant information down in one place. Looking at the initial mind map shows what areas are weak and need more research.

+ Planning. Using a mind map also helps organize the material so it can easily be turned into a formal outline, and then into a paper: All the information is grouped under headings and subheadings. All that's necessary is to decide in which sequence to present the ideas.

Mind maps can be used for planning any piece of writing, from a letter to a screenplay to a book (I used a master map for this whole book, and a detailed submap for each chapter), or for planning a meeting, a day, or a vacation.

If you'd like to try using a mind map before having your students do this, there is a passage to read at: http://www.coun.uvic.ca/learn/program/hndouts/class1.html. Then you can compare your mind map with the one at http://www.coun.uvic.ca/learn/program/hndouts/class1a.html (note: This map does not have images on it, just words, branches, and arrows). There is also software called Inspiration that my students and I have used to create mind maps; it's great, especially if you're not really good at drawing things. You can download a free trial package at http://www.inspiration.com/general_biz.html.

One final thought on mind maps: Tony Buzan (1989) notes, "Using these techniques at Oxford University, students were able to complete essays in one third of the previous time, while receiving higher marks" (p.102).

KWLH

This is like a standard KWL, but with a twist. Fold a blank paper into four columns instead of three. Label one column K for Know; another, W for Want to know; a third, L for Learned; and the fourth, H, for How we can learn more.

As a hook before reading, announce the topic or theme of the reading and have students list in the K section, in the target language, what they already know. If the story takes place in Madrid, they could list what they know about Madrid: places, customs, foods, and so on. If the characters are students, they could list vocabulary about school and studies.

As the students do the K section, they should also think of things to put in the W (Want to know) section, in English: vocabulary they think they'll need, questions they have about the topic, and so on.

Then, as they read, they fill in, opposite the Wants, the information they find: vocabulary words, answers to the questions, and more questions or reflections (favorite quotes, new unanticipated vocabulary, or customs, etc.).

Finally, in the H section, they think of resources for learning more on the topic, to get answers to any questions in the L section or to follow up an idea that interested them.

Reader's Theater

An oral reading activity much like an old-fashioned radio drama, Reader's Theater has students become characters in books and stories. Because it involves repeated reading (out loud and silently), Reader's Theater stimulates fluency in reading, improves reading skills, and helps reluctant readers engage a text in a fun way (it's gratifying when the class applauds and they get compliments). Reader's Theater can be done with nonfiction (especially history) and with biographies as well as fiction.

Begin by choosing a story or passage that has a lot of dialogue. Convert it into a play script by indicating speakers' names and by adding a narrator for the nondialogue portions. Some teachers like to put the text in clear plastic folder pages; then students can use an overhead marker or a highlighter to indicate their dialogue portion, making the text into a script.

Tips for Reader's Theater

♦ Use small groups, no more than four. In a typical dialogue, there are only two speakers. So, there would be two (sometimes three) speakers and one or two narrators.

♦ Practice, practice, practice! Have the student read first for rate and fluency before they work on interpretation (e.g., whispering, emotional tone). This will build confidence. Students may also need coaching on how to use punctuation marks to pause and breathe. They may need to mark places to take breaths in the script. Send scripts home for individual practice. Allow small groups to rehearse alone or with your help. Coach students on giving helpful rather than harsh critiques of one another's performance skills.

♦ Know your character. To improve oral interpretation, make sure students know their characters' emotions and intentions. Have students contrast their characters: mean and sweet, and so on. This will make it easier for them to change their voices and put some real feeling into what could otherwise be lifeless.

♦ Have an audience, but only a small one. The audience should never have the script, but just listen and respond. You may need to coach the audience on proper, respectful responses.

WebQuests

A really good way to bring students into contact with authentic readings, information, and culture is to have them surf the Internet to find information on a topic of their choice (differentiated content) or on a topic of the teacher's choice but with a product chosen by the student. WebQuests are described in more detail (with examples) in Chapter 4. A really good source for WebQuests already written and ready to go is http://trackstar.4teachers.org, and an excellent source for projects, tutorials, and good sites if you're writing your own WebQuest is Blue Web'n: http://www.kn.pacbell.com/wired/bluewebn.

Jigsaw: Read a Novel in an Hour

Jigsaw is a Cooperative Learning strategy in which students are split into small "expert groups" that do an activity (or several) and report back to the rest of the class. If you find yourself pressed for time at the end of a grading period because of weather, illness, or other circumstances, this is the strategy for you. If you have a group of reluctant readers, this strategy is perfect. Use a novel with short, action-oriented chapters for best results.

I have to say that this method's title refers to reading a book in *English* and that in a foreign language I find an hour is just not enough. But it *is* a quick way to fit a novel in your curriculum, if you've never found time before to do so.

In this strategy, a book is divided into small parts (one or two chapters). If you can afford to be really dramatic, physically rip apart a book and hand a section to each group. Each group reads only that section, after which the class meets for a whole-class reporting and discussion. Each group should be given the following tasks:

♦ Reading their section, individually or as a group (remember, give choices!), and then determining the most important thing in their portion

♦ Agreeing on the main idea

♦ Preparing a clear summary for the class

I have my own twist on this method. I never give the last chapter to any group (although I find many voluntarily read it on their own time), and I always start the questions with the group that had the beginning of the book and give my students a graphic to fill out as the chapters are discussed. Then, for closure, we all read the final chapter of the book as a group.

I also know someone who hands out random, unnumbered chapters of a children's book to individual students. During discussion, she then asks students if they think their chapter is at the beginning, middle, or end of the book. She chooses someone who thinks his or her chapter is first, has them give their report, and then asks for someone who thinks theirs is next, and so on. By the end of the discussion, the class has reassembled the book. (By the way, many students then want to read the whole book from cover to cover.)

Literature Circles

This is a strategy related to Jigsaw, but with each group reading a different book together. Each group gets a packet of materials: vocabulary lists to assist in comprehension, plus several work sheets to complete. Then they are free to come up with their own plans to ensure that every person in the group reads and understands the story. I suggest having students fill out a log as they read. The display on page 134 is an example.

Literature Circles Discussion Log

Title and author: _____

Pages: _____   Date of discussion: _____

Journal (jot down thoughts while reading, with the page number of the section
    you are reacting to): _____

_____

_____

_____

Part that I'd like to share with the group (write the first and last words and page
    numbers):

One question I have about the reading:

Selected vocabulary words (choose at least two):

Checklist: Are you ready?
    ☐ I finished the assigned reading.
    ☐ I put my best effort into the work.
    ☐ I added the vocabulary to my big list.
    ☐ I completed this form.
    ☐ I marked the parts I want to share.

The group must discuss the story. Guideline statements:

- ♦ I thought…
- ♦ I liked…
- ♦ I wonder…
- ♦ I felt…

The group must present a skit based on a scene from the book, or some other short project, to the class on a given report date.

Colleagues report that the small-group setting makes each individual participate more actively, because he or she feels more accountable. They also report that there's a more informal and relaxed atmosphere in which work seems more enjoyable for both students and teacher.

Below are a variety of questions to use in student packets or discussions.

Literature Circle Questions

- ♦ In what ways might the author have…?
- ♦ What are all the words used to…?
- ♦ How many different…are there?
- ♦ What are the main ideas in…?
- ♦ Give an example of…?
- ♦ How is (character) like…?
- ♦ Why is (character) like…?
- ♦ What if…?
- ♦ What do you think would happen if…?
- ♦ Why do you suppose…happened in the story?
- ♦ Why do you suppose the writer…?
- ♦ Would you rather be…or…?
- ♦ Would you like to be…? Why or why not?
- ♦ What if this book were told from the viewpoint of…?
- ♦ If you were (character), what would you do?
- ♦ What are some different ways (main character) could have solved the problem(s) in this story?
- ♦ What would happen if this story were set in (a different time or place)?
- ♦ How would the story change if (main character) were a different gender?

- How would the story change if (main character) were (a different nationality)?

- Suggest a different ending for this story.

- If you were making this into a movie, who would you cast as (main characters)?

- If you were making this into a movie, what scenes would you leave out?

- If you were making this into a movie, what might you want to change?

Poetry Gallery

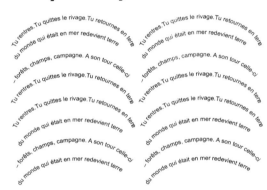

Begin by choosing a number of age-appropriate and engaging poems. As a French teacher, I often use Calligrammes, a sort of picture poem (see example) as a first Poetry Gallery walk. Copy and enlarge each poem and mount it on paper, number it, and post it on the wall of the classroom at approximately eye level. Give each student several Post-it notes.

Then perform a think-aloud reading of one of the poems, showing students what you would like them to do (your choice: read aloud, look for rhymes, write a personal reflection, suggest changes, find similes or metaphors, or whatever you'd have them look for). Write down whatever reaction you have, what helped you understand the poem, and so on, and post it for other students.

Have students count off (in the target language, of course) up to the number of poems, so each has a poem to begin at (this avoids having large groups at the closest one). Explain the rules for the walk: no talking, how many poems total each student should read (usually one for each Post-it; after the first poem, I let them choose the others themselves), what to do if they finish quickly, and how much time they have.

Have students begin to walk through the Gallery. Play some mellow music quietly to enhance an atmosphere of genteel reflection. When the time is up, have students take their seats, and do whatever follow-up activity you would like. They might, with a partner, pick a poem to write a short reflection on, or write a similar poem themselves, alone or with a group (their choice!), or you might like to have a group discussion or do another follow-up reading project of your choice.

Postreading Projects and Strategies

Again, there are the obvious standard activities: a trivia competition (Jeopardy, Millionaire, or other game-show format), a closed- or open-book test, a student critique of the book (book report), or a wrap-up Socratic discussion. The following sections contain some other ideas.

More Standard Activities

Story Box

Have students place loose items in a box. Each item must represent one of the aspects of the story: setting, characters, plot, and so on. They should do a show-and-tell presentation to explain why they chose these objects and how they relate to the story.

Sales Pitch

The sales pitch can be either oral or written—sell the story as a good one to make into a movie.

Key Verbs List

Students should carefully choose 10 verbs—no synonyms allowed—that illustrate what occurred in the story.

Illustrations

This is a really good strategy for students who have special learning problems or who are incredibly artistic. They can draw things like the following suggestions:

♦ An obstacle course that shows the main character's progress throughout the story (*Don Quixote, Young Werther, Candide, The Little Prince*).

♦ A similar idea: a game board with rules and playing pieces, like Candy Land or Life, based on the reading and showing events from the story.

♦ A character chart, much like a solar system, with the main character in the center. Give students the option of choosing shapes that might tell something about the character or the relationship. For example, the main character could be a star, something prickly looking, a square, or an arrow. Then list the other characters he or she is closest to in the closest shapes; all shapes would be connected to the main character by solid or dotted lines (dotted to indicate former relationships that no longer exist).

♦ A drawing of items named in the story, in the order they are named (a good graphic to help remember the plot).

♦ A rebus story: a plot summary—in which pictures take the place of many of the words—that can be read aloud (or silently) to review the story line.

♦ Two posters—one with the first sentence and the other with the last sentence of the story—each with visuals showing the main character, the setting, the atmosphere, and key events from the story.

♦ A cartoonlike storyboard of events, with drawings, dialogue, and labels.

♦ A mobile with dangling pictures and symbols, accompanied by a brief oral or written presentation to explain what they are and why they were chosen.

♦ A T-shirt painted or stamped with information on the topic, accompanied by a brief oral or written presentation of it and what it represents.

♦ A perfect Halloween-time take on a book report: tombstones for all characters, with a symbol for each and a brief explanation of who they were and what they did. (Think of having more advanced students do poems similar to those in Edgar Lee Masters's *Spoon River Anthology* (a good connection to make with English class content, perhaps for team teaching).

Speaking

♦ Act out events and have the class guess which scene it is.

♦ Perform a skit in which various characters from the book have a conversation about a topic of students' choice: a theme from the book, a current event, an event in the book, and so on.

♦ Create a talk show or a news interview of one of the characters in the book.

♦ Act out a trial of one of the characters in the book.

Writing

♦ Write conversations with or between various characters.

♦ Make a scrapbook (drawings, news clippings, or magazine photos plus "snapshot writing" of six short "word pictures").

♦ Double-entry journal: Have students keep a journal while they read, using paper with a line drawn down the center.

Here is what one might look like:

Left-Hand Side	Right-Hand Side

Quotes from reading	Visual commentary:
	  Drawings
	  Doodles
	Written reactions, reflections, comments
	  (race, class, gender inequalities, etc.)
	Questions (clarifying, probing)
	Connections:
	  Text to another text
	  Text to self
	  Text to world (current or past events)
	Significance of quote
	Why the text says the quoted portion
	Memories
	Listing literary techniques
	  (metaphors, etc.)

"I wonder why" comments	Possible answers: "Because…"

♦ "Somebody/Wanted/But/So" activity. Students write a sentence for each of the following:

- Somebody—Identify the main character in the story.
- Wanted—Identify the problem in the story.
- But—Identify obstacles to solving the problem.
- So—Tell the solution or outcome.

Here are some more ideas for follow-up projects to do after reading, many of which involve writing:

♦ Newspaper article
♦ Video news report
♦ Editorial cartoon
♦ Caricatures of key figures
♦ Storyboard
♦ Treaties, agreements, contracts
♦ Mock trial
♦ Debate
♦ Letter to the editor
♦ Letter to the author
♦ Letter from one character to another
♦ Videotaped or written investigative report

♦ Testimonial video
♦ Reenactment (skit or video)
♦ Book cover
♦ Town meeting
♦ Point/counterpoint
♦ Interview of main character (written or oral)
♦ Advice column written by main character
♦ Photo essay
♦ Puppet show
♦ Poem

Many more projects may be found in the display at the end of the chapter (page 156).

Writing

We all know the standard forms used for writing in the classroom:

Answering questions	Note taking
Book reports	Poetry
Copying from the board or book	Preparations for oral presentations
Dialogues and scripts	Research papers
Essays	Short stories
Journaling	Summaries
Letters	Workbook pages

Here are some less familiar ways to ask students to write:

Everyday Texts

Every language teacher tries to incorporate authentic texts for students to read, but how many of us have students write them? Having students write an everyday text teaches important lessons about reading and writing. Close, critical reading will show students how texts attempt to appeal to readers' race, gender, age, and class and to influence their attitudes. Writing an everyday text makes students aware of considerations such as audience, voice, and choosing the right word (diction). Here is a list of everyday texts you could ask students to write.

Everyday Texts

Acrostic	Do's and don'ts	Homily	Letter to the editor
Advertisement	Editorial	Horoscope	Lie
Board game	E-mail	How-to	List
Book review	Epitaph	Hyperbole	Log
Bumper sticker	Eulogy	Idiom	Lost and found
Cartoon	Excuse note	Instructions	Map
Chat-room	Fable	Interview	Missing poster
message	Form to be filled out	Invitation	Movie review
Code	Friendly letter	Joke	Myth
Commercial	Graffiti	Journal	Narrative
Confession	Greeting card	Lab report	Note
Consumer report	Grocery list	Laws	Obituary
Deposition	Haiku	Legend	Outline
Diary	Headline		Parable

Parody	Proposal	Script	To-do list
Personal ad	Psalm	Sketch	Wanted poster
Persuasive essay	Question	Slang dialogue	Weather report
Phone message	Ransom note	Song	Wedding
Police report	Real estate ad	Survey	announcement
Prediction	Recipe	Tall tale	Will
Propaganda	Report card	Tattoo	
Proverb	Riddle	Testimony	

Invitation

Everybody likes a party! Have students practice interrogatives by creating a party invitation (*quinceañera*, birthday, or any holiday).

- ◆ Who?
- ◆ What?
- ◆ Where?
- ◆ When?
- ◆ Why?

Flip Books

These are an interesting way to force students to read, decide what's important in what they've read, and reduce it to a manageable text. It is sort of a low-tech PowerPoint presentation, with each page of the book showing a different fact or aspect of a subject.

How to Create a Flip Book

Take three sheets of paper. Cut them in half lengthwise ("hot dog," if you know the "hamburger/hot dog" folds).

Align the three sheets, one on top of the others. Move the top sheet so that its bottom edge is about a half inch above the bottom edge of the middle sheet. Keeping the top sheet in place, carefully move the middle sheet so its bottom edge is about a half inch above the bottom edge of the last sheet.

Leaving the staggered bottom edges in place, bend the three sheets in about the middle, toward you, so there are now six flip book pages, each about a half inch above the next.

When you have evened out the pages as much as possible, fold and crease the top edge of all three sheets to form the flip book. Secure the pages in place by putting several staples just below the fold. Your book will be about eight and a half to nine inches tall.

There are now six pages (or 12, if you have students use the backs as well); the top page is the cover, so have students decide what five types of information are in the chapter (if this is a chapter-review flip book) or what five (or 10, if the students are using the backs) categories of information they intend to use to tell about their subject (for a flip book on a famous person or a country, city, or monument). I usually have them do a mind map or fill out a graphic organizer so I can see their thoughts are well organized. Then students transfer that information to their flip books, adding cover art and illustrations as time permits.

This can easily become a modified SQ3R activity: with five pages, one can be Survey, and another can be Question, followed by Read, Recite, and Review. Somehow it's more fun as a flip book than as a graphic. (See the section on reading for more specifics on the SQ3R method).

Another Type of Flip Book

To give students lots of practice writing sentences and to really make them aware of sentence order (where adjectives and adverbs go), try this type of flip book: Cut several sheets of paper in fourths, and staple them together along one long side like a book.

Then take scissors and cut into seven strips (six cuts) parallel to the short edges, most of the way through to the stapled part. Then have students write sentence pieces on each set of flaps (for French):

- ♦ On the left (or at the top) write names or nouns.
- ♦ On the one next to it, adjectives.
- ♦ On the third set, verbs in the infinitive.
- ♦ On the next, adverbs.
- ♦ On the fifth, more nouns (will serve as direct or indirect objects).
- ♦ On the sixth, more adjectives.
- ♦ On the seventh, prepositional phrases: how, where, when.

Have students use their own books or exchange them, flip the flaps, and write a certain number of sentences, no matter how absurd (those can be quite amusing).

Have them write their favorite one on the board.

Little Books

Turn one piece of paper into a 10-page book in this way:

Take one 8½ × 11 sheet of paper. Fold it lengthwise ("hot dog"), then in half and in half again. Open it up completely. There will be eight sections. Cut a slit along the hot dog crease in the two center sections:

The cut goes along line A, between pages 1 and 6 and pages 2 and 5.

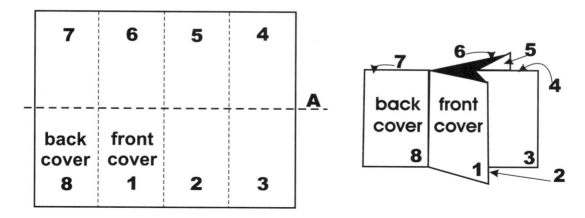

Refold along line A, and holding sections 7 and 8 and 3 and 4, push those sections together. The slit will pop open. Continue to move page 3 inward, and fold the pages over so the cover (1) and back (8) are on the outside.

You now have a Little Book. I often give students the option (tiered assignments, a grid, learning centers, etc.) of making a Little Book for topics of their own choosing or any of the following:

- Seasons
- Months
- Colors
- Reflexive verbs
- Family
- Favorite foods
- Sports and equipment

- An island and things to do and see there
- Eating healthy
- A sight in a city the class is studying
- An illustrated chapter vocabulary
- Rooms in a house
- Adjectives

Blogging

A relatively new concept is a classroom Web log, a sort of online bulletin board; Web logs, or blogs for short, are becoming increasingly popular as a way to encourage students to write. Blogs are a space on the Internet where students can carry on conversations and post stories and poems or even pictures; they're very simple to make, use, and maintain. Teachers who use blogs say that students put a lot more thought and effort into their blog writing, knowing that parents and others may read their work on the Web. A free site to make a blog for your classroom is http://www.blogger.com.

You could have students maintain a blog paired with an English class in a country that speaks the target language. They could post in English and your students could comment on their postings in English; your students could post in the TL, and the foreign students would comment in that language—sort of like an e-mail conversation, but it's there for everyone to see.

You could also put students in groups and have them post to a group blog for conversation practice. They could post rough drafts of a report for comments, write a story together in which each adds a piece, give one another compliments, talk about likes and dislikes; there are thousands of possibilities.

Cornell Note Taking

The Cornell system for taking notes is designed to make it easier to organize and review notes, as well as to save time by not making students recopy them. However, I have found that only students who are already skilled at taking notes do this well; less-skilled students do better with a graphic organizer or other form of scaffolding that shows them exactly where to put specific information.

First, prepare your paper by dividing it into three sections, as shown in this display.

Cornell Note-Taking Format

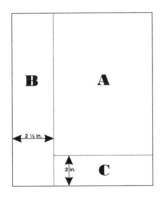

Part A is where you start, by taking notes, not in exact words, but condensed to essential information, using whatever system you like.

Then go to area B, as soon as possible after the lecture, and write questions about A next to where the answers are in the notes. For example, next to notes on how to form the imperfect tense, you would write "How do you make the imperfect?"

Finally, in area C, you write a summary, no more than three sentences long, of the material in area A.

Then, when you're ready to review the material, just cover up parts A and C and try to answer the questions you wrote in part B. If you're an oral learner, do it out loud.

Here's an example for a Spanish lesson.

Statements of equality
   tan/como
     examples
 	
   tanto/como
     examples
 	
   tanto/a   tantos/as
	Saying something is equal to, the same as
	Use with adjectives
	   (examples)
	   (examples)
	Use with nouns
	Has to agree in gender and number with nouns
	   (examples)
	   (examples)

	(examples) (examples)

The students can fold the page on the break between left and right and study the main concepts without seeing the details. It can also be used like a Ladders sheet (see the section on vocabulary review, below) for pair study, because one partner sees the details and the other sees the main concepts.

For part C (the bottom), the obvious use might be to write sample sentences, using those phrases, or to rewrite the explanation in sentence form and tell how or when you'd use it as homework for the next day.

This method also works well for vocabulary if you have the students put the TL word in a sentence (I like to teach in context) on the left and definitions and pictures on the right.

RAFT Assignment

RAFT is a writing system that makes sure students understand what their Role, Audience, Format, and Topic are. It is always based on unit objectives and standards and makes a writing assignment much easier for less-than-gifted students. Practically all RAFT writing is done from a fictional viewpoint. This display is an example of a RAFT assignment I use for a foods unit.

Sample RAFT Assignment: Foods Unit

Role	*Audience*	*Format*	*Topic*
Cookbook writer	Cooks	Recipe	Instructions on food preparation
Chef	Customer	Menu	Detailed description of food preparation
Customer	Restaurant owner	Complaint	Problem with food or poor service
Travel writer	Reader wanting to travel	Recommendation	Good things to eat while in France, and what to avoid
Student overseas	Parents	Letter	Staying with a family; you describe a typical meal
Pick one of the above situations, pick up a checklist for that particular task, and use the Internet, Microsoft Publisher, and any other source to make your work look real.			

Checklists

The following checklists are for French; you may need to tweak them for other languages. Each criterion gets two points.

Recipe
Prewriting:

☐ Before writing a recipe, consider looking at recipes online or in the cookbooks on the back shelf of the classroom.

☐ Decide if you're going to make an hors d'oeuvre, a main dish, a dessert, or an item from another category.

☐ Think up a name for your recipe.

Writing:

☐ Write all in French.

☐ The verbs should be in infinitive form.

☐ Include at least six ingredients.

☐ Use the metric system used for measurements (and so on).

☐ There should be no spelling errors.

☐ The recipe format should be realistic.

Menu
Prewriting:

☐ Before writing a menu, look at sample restaurant menus from the folder.

☐ Decide what main categories you'll have (meat, fish, salad, sandwiches, etc.).

☐ Foods must have a description (ingredients; preparation, such as baked or fried; etc.).

☐ You'll need a name and a logo for your restaurant.

☐ The menu should be all in French.

☐ Prices should be given for each item.

☐ The menu should be no longer than two pages.

☐ There should be no spelling errors.

☐ The menu format should be realistic.

Complaint
Prewriting:

☐ Decide on a date, a salutation, and a closing.

☐ Pick a restaurant name, the owner's name, the date of the bad experience.

☐ Be ready to name specific items eaten and describe them.

☐ Suggest an action to take regarding this complaint.

Writing:

☐ The letter should be all in French.

☐ Use complete sentences.

☐ There should be no spelling errors.

☐ Use both past tenses and present tense (future is optional).

Recommendation

Prewriting:

☐ Invent a restaurant name, a location, hours, the chef's name (the owner's name is optional).

☐ Select a date of experience; name specific items eaten.

☐ Decide on the theme (e.g., Mexico, pirates, Snoopy, racing) and the ambience of the restaurant (table settings, décor, etc.).

☐ Award stars for a good meal and tell why or why not stars were awarded.

Writing:

☐ The recommendation should be all in French.

☐ Use complete sentences.

☐ Use adjectives ("delicious," "spicy," etc.).

☐ There should be no spelling errors.

☐ Use both past tenses and present tense (future is optional).

Letter to Parents

Rough draft:

☐ The rough draft should be written in standard letter form: date, salutation, closing.

☐ Use past tense to describe food you have eaten.

☐ Use present tense to describe foods you like or don't like.

☐ Tell something you will eat in future.

☐ Tell a little bit about table manners you used or observed being used.

☐ The draft should be all in French.

☐ Use complete sentences.

☐ There should be no spelling errors.

There are more generic checklists in Chapter 6 on assessments for other types of assignments you might use for a RAFT.

Fairy Tales

"Once upon a time," "*Erase una vez*," "*Il était une fois*"—all languages have a phrase like this. That's because all children love stories. Have your students practice the different past tenses by writing a 10-sentence fairy tale, using an organizer. (This should be in the target language.)

Once upon a time there lived _____.

His/her/their name(s) was/were _____.

He/she/they were _____.

He/she/they had _____.

They did not have _____.

They wanted to _____.

So they went to _____.

They met _____.

They fought _____.

At last, they _____.

Using an organizer makes the task seem more manageable. This can be done even in level 1 classes, if instead of blanks you give students a list of words to choose from.

Writing a fairy tale allows students to use some unusual vocabulary, and they can also illustrate the story, act it out, read it to other students, and so on.

ABC Book

An ABC book can be done at any level. Fold seven sheets of paper in half hamburger style (for French I usually use only six, because as we omit K and W, which don't have many words to choose from) and staple it along the fold. After cover art, each page will have one letter of the alphabet with a word that begins with that letter and an illustration of it.

At level 2, the illustration is accompanied by a sentence (e.g., M—Mouse. The mouse is in the house). At level 3, the students must choose a theme, such as cities, animals, things in a house, and find words to fit it.

Review

Vocabulary Practice

Flash Cards

Flash cards are probably a most-used individual or group method of practice and, before a test, review. But did you know that there are online programs to make them? A Web site that lets you make your own electronic flash cards is at http://www.flashcardmachine.com.

What can you do with flash cards? Other than having students just go through them individually, you could have them, with one partner, quiz each other, seeing who can get them all right in the fewest rounds. They can put correctly answered cards in a pile and mix up the missed ones. Pairs could play Concentration: combine their sets, TL side down and with a blank piece on top if they are two-sided, and turn up two at a time to try to match them. With three or more partners, they could play Go Fish: combine their sets, deal them like cards, hold them with just the tops peeking over their fingers, and ask another player for a certain card.

Ladders

This is one of my students' favorite vocabulary games. To play, have your students prepare a Ladders sheet. (I used to do this for them until I let them have more choice in their vocabulary lists. I still do them with my nonnegotiable vocabulary.)

1. Fold a paper in half, hot dog style (vertically).
2. On the left half, list vocabulary words for the unit, with the hardest ones on top and the easiest on the bottom.
3. On the right half, opposite each word, list either a drawing or its English equivalent.

To play Ladders, two students sit together with one Ladders sheet. First they decide whether they want to practice drawing from TL to English or vice versa. Then, starting on the bottom word (to climb a ladder, one starts at the bottom), student A begins saying the equivalent while student B looks at the answer and gives him or her feedback on whether he or she was correct. If student A is correct, he or she does the one above it, trying to climb to the top of the ladder. If student A misses one, he or she has "fallen off" the ladder, the paper is turned around, and student B tries to climb it. If student B falls, student A gets another chance, starting from the bottom once again. Whoever gets to the top first wins.

Password and Taboo

Have students look at categories for vocabulary from the chapter. A given chapter often has more than one category—for example, a chapter on the house could have categories such as floors (attic, basement, ground floor, etc.), rooms, furniture (which can be divided into things to sit on, things to put stuff on, things made of wood, etc.) décor (posters, curtains, rugs, flowers), plumbing and built-in items (tub, closet), and appliances.

To play Password, at a signal one person would give a partner, or a group, the category and then a clue—which does not use a form of the word itself—to induce them to name the items listed for that category, in the order they are listed. For example, if the category is rooms, a good clue might be "sleep" for bedroom, but a bad clue would be "bed." If the game is played within a group, individual students take turns guessing, and each gets a different clue. For each item they can name before time is up, they get a point. If the game is played between two groups, both have the same list, and group leaders alternate giving clues to their group until one group gets the answer.

To play Taboo, at a signal one person uses the vocabulary list and any other clues they can devise to get their partner or partners to discover the category itself. This is good for almost any vocabulary, such as colors, family members, school supplies, classes, health, body parts, weather, months, and verbs.

Verb Practice

If practicing conjugation and endings is your goal, rather than the verb's meaning, try one of these the following activities

Patty-Cake

Just as with the children's game, each student has a partner. (They can also do it with the top of their desks, but it's not as educational or fun. Still, I give students a choice of one or the other.) Have them say a verb as they slap their lap, and then hold up their hands about shoulder height, palms facing the partner. As they clap their hands in front of themselves, they say a subject (pronoun or noun) and then return to the palm-outward position. Whenever they know the verb form for that subject, they slap their left palm against their partner's left palm, saying it aloud at the same time. Then back to clap, next pronoun, and then slap right palms together as they say the verb form for that pronoun.

Imagine (example in Spanish): (slap lap) *leer* (clap) *yo* (slap left hands) *leo* (clap) *tu* (slap right hands) *lees* (clap) *el* (slap left hands) *lee* (clap) *ella* (slap right hands) *lee,* and so on through the verb. If a student doesn't know it, he or she can listen to the partner and repeat it before slapping. (This is the disadvantage of allowing students to slap their desks instead of a partner's hand.) Have them try to go faster and faster or work their way down through a given list of verbs.

Magic Number Roll 'n' Rock

This is my students' favorite verb review game. Having the students clear their desks except for a blank sheet of paper. Group them in threes or fours, and have them decide who will begin. Give each group one pen and one die and a list of verbs (or list them on the board, overhead transparency, or TV screen, or they could select a certain number of verbs from the chapter).

At your signal, the first person in each group starts rolling the die until he or she gets a six (or whatever number you tell them). Once the student gets that number, he or she picks up the pen and begins conjugating the verb on his paper. As soon as the player lays down the die to pick up the pen, the student next to him throws the die, trying to get the Magic Number. When that student gets it, he or she grabs the pen from the first student's hand and begins conjugating while the next student rolls frantically to get the Magic Number, and so on. One student is always rolling and one is writing, and the game is very fast paced.

It would be easy to modify this to practice vocabulary words.

Creator

This activity is very simple but fun. Have students create their own verbs and conjugate them and teach their meanings and conjugations to a group or class. This is a good way to practice regular verb endings. Encourage the students to be creative and to use humor.

Verb Turkey

We usually end a grading period with a big exam around Thanksgiving, so to review, students make "hand turkeys" like those in grade school (the thumb gets a beak and wattle, to become the turkey's head), outlining their hand but adding two extra fingers. Then each student writes a verb in the infinitive form on the turkey's body, and gives the turkey props, dialogue, or a setting to suggest the verb's meaning. For example, for the "to swim," the student could give the turkey a bathing cap and water to stand in. Then, on each finger feather, students write a subject pronoun and the correct form of the verb. After you check the turkeys for accuracy, put them up in the room and do a Gallery Walk for students to see and review.

Whole-Chapter Practice

Learning Centers

I post questions or activities around the room for students to do to review a chapter. Examples of learning centers:

- Name three things out loud found in a (backpack, bedroom, makeup kit, pastry shop, etc.).

- Tell how you (make this list of adjectives feminine, change a verb into the imperfect tense, hold a fork and knife, and so on).

- Look at the paper on the wall at this site. (Have students write something and put their initials next to it.) For example, on a question-writing chapter, it might say: "If the last thing written is a question, answer it" or "If the last thing written is an answer, read the paper and write a question that hasn't been asked yet." If it's a shopping chapter, you might have them write a typical dialogue between shopper and shopkeeper, one line at a time. It could be a room in a house; each student needs to add an item found there that hasn't been written yet. Or the students have to name a food in a particular category, such as "green" or "eaten hot."

- ◆ Take turns timing one another and checking for accuracy as you match the cards correctly. (Have a picture on one and a vocabulary word on the other, for example, such as a clock and the time written in words.)

- ◆ Put on the headphones, listen to the tape, and write what is being said. Then pick up the card with the star on it and check what you've written.

- ◆ Read the (realia item such as an ad or a menu) and answer the questions on the card taped next to it.

- ◆ Go to the teacher and tell her _____.

I always try to make the learning-center activities provide practice in the exact skills used on the test. If there's a reading on the test, one center has the students read. If they must speak, use the tell-the-teacher type of activity. If there's a listening section, have a tape or CD practice. If they need to construct a dialogue or list items, for example, make sure you have a center for that skill. Number each center, and assign students a number to ensure they don't all start at the same spot. If the next number is busy, tell them to skip it and return to it. Have them write on a piece of scrap paper the number of centers and cross each number off (or write their contribution, time, response, or whatever on a sheet of paper) to help them remember which sites they've already visited and which they still need to do. (Have an anchor activity for early finishers!)

Send-a-Problem

This activity is for both individual and team practice.

Decide how many teams of three or four you will have. For each team, prepare a page like that represented in the display on the following page. Each paper will be either numbered or lettered or a different color of paper so each team's is unique in some way. If you want to do a permanent version, put a similar grid on poster board and have it laminated. Make the left column about two inches, the right one about three inches, and the center section the largest.

Send-a-Problem Blank

Create as many sentences as there are blanks on the grid times the number of teams: five blanks and five teams = 25 sentences. (I save mine on the computer so I can cut down on preparation time the next time I do the unit, of course.) The sentences should focus on whatever structure will be tested. They might have students translate from one language to another or assemble sentence pieces in order or convert a word list into a sentence to practice verb conjugations. Cut the sentences into strips, and tape a few to each team's sheet so they can be lifted like flaps.

Round 1: Each group gets a paper and one colored marker (each team has its own color) and writes the names of the team members on it. On scrap paper, each of them silently does the team's first sentence. When all are done, they compare answers and decide which ones are correct and why. Students must correct their answers. Then one of the group will lift the flap and pencil in lightly the agreed-upon group answer (it must not be easily visible). This procedure is repeated for the remaining sentences until all are done, and everyone has his or her corrected paper to keep.

Round 2: Have the groups exchange papers with a different group. Without looking, they follow the same procedure (doing the problems silently and comparing and correcting), but this time they lift the flap and see what the other team answered. If they like it, they draw something positive in the third column (e.g., smiley face, rainbow, star, piece of candy). If they don't like it, they draw something negative (e.g., frown, roadkill, bolt of lightning—emphasize it should be class-appropriate!)

Round 3: See instructions for Round 2. I teach on block schedule, and we have time for three rounds before the final one. It is also possible to do Round 1 on one day, and the rest of the activity the following day.

Final Round: Each group gets back its own paper and looks at the pictures drawn. If they get a negative drawing, they try to figure out what they did wrong, and if they can't, they send a representative to the other group (they can tell who by the marker color) for help.

This is a good activity, because by observing, I get feedback on what problems they are still having and because students have to perform to please their peers and you get the student-teaching-student dynamic that brain research says results in the best retention of any teaching strategy. Also, because of the gamelike structure, this activity is good for team building and class morale.

Don't forget to have a sponge or anchor activity ready, because groups will finish at different times.

Other

Are you as tired as I am of always seeing the same four or five formats for project reports? My students were always doing posters or PowerPoint presentations, written papers, or time lines. Encourage them to try the following:

Storytelling

Using voice, gestures, dialogue, and so on (even pictures, and audience participation, such as holding up pictures or making sound effects), make the report into a story. In Africa, there is a technique, called cric-crac, in which the storyteller pauses every so often and asks, "Cric?" (pronounced *creek*) to which the listeners reply "Crac!" to have them continue the story. This makes the listener a more active participant and gives the speaker a chance to take a breath, turn the page, check notes, or whatever.

Creative Writing

This includes poems, raps, or short stories using the topic as a character, a setting, or an event.

Photojournalism

Examples are family books, photos from the Internet, or digital pictures of friends acting out elements of the report, accompanied by text.

Sales Pitch

Sell the class on the topic—they should want to vote for it, buy it, use it, read it.

Drama

Put on a skit or make a film.

Seminar

Have a student lead a class discussion. Or assign students in the audience specific questions to ask of "the expert" and take notes on the answers.

Web Sites

Students can create a WebQuest or just a page with links to readings on the topic they have chosen.

Graphics

Whether it's painting, photography, or illustration—students create an art work that's a copy of a famous painting or done in a typical traditional style, for example.

Community-Service Projects

This could include illustrating paper bags on healthy eating for a local grocery or performing a song or skit for a nursing home audience.

Model or Display

A student can demonstrate how to make something—a food, a craft—or display an item, such as native dress, a music video or part of a movie, or a realia item obtained by travel or by writing to a travel bureau.

Crafts

These include *papel picado, ojos de dios,* weaving, piñatas, castanets, rain sticks, *cascarones,* bark painting, paper flowers (Spanish), and masks (almost every language group has traditional masks for a particular holiday or ceremony).

Here is a list of my ABCs of products for further inspiration. For a list of product ideas connected to Gardner's intelligences, see page 182.

ABCs of Products

A
action plan
adventure
advertisement
advice column
album
anagram
analysis of samples
anecdote
animation
apparatus
artifact collection
audiotape recording
autobiography
anecdote
award

B
ballad
ballet
banner
biographical presentation
bio-poem
block picture story
blueprints
book
book jacket
booklet
bookmark
book report
brainteaser
brochure
bullet chart
bulletin board
business letter

C
calendar
campaign speech
caption
card game
cartoon
CD cover
celebrity profile
ceramic
charade
chart
characterization
checklist
children's book
choral reading
cinquain
classified ad
clothing
collage
collection
comedy act
comic book
commentary
commercial
comparison
computer program
conversation
costume
couplet
coupon
creative writing
critique
crossword puzzle

D
dance
debate

demonstration
description
design a structure (e.g.,
   new product or new
   animal)
diagram
dialogue
diary
dictionary entry
diorama
directions
discussion
display
documentary
dramatization
drawing

E
editorial
editorial cartoon
equipment
essay
etching
exaggeration
exhibit
explanation
eyewitness account

F
fabric
fairy tale
field trip
film
finger puppet(s)
flag
flannel board
flash cards

flip chart
flowchart
food
free verse
friendly letter
furniture

G
gadget
gallery
game
glossary
gossip column
graph
graphic organizer
greeting card
guidebook

H
haiku
hand puppet
handbook
handout
hat
headline
hieroglyphic
history
hypothesis

I
illustration
imprint
instrument
interior monologue
interview
invention
invitation

J
jigsaw puzzle
jingle
job description
joke
journal

K
kite
kitsch

L
law
learning center
lecture
lesson plan
letter
letter of complaint (e.g.,
  opinion, request,
  support, to editor)
limerick
list
log
lyrics

M
machine
macramé
magazine article
manual
map
marionette
mask
memorandum
mentor
metaphor
mime
mnemonic
mobile
mock trial
model
monologue
montage
monument
mosaic
movement
multimedia
mural
music
musical
myth

N
narration

needlework
newscast
newsletter
newspaper
newspaper ad
newspaper article
new story ending
notes
nursery rhyme

O
oath
observation
oral report
origami
order form
outline

P
painting
pamphlet
panel discussion
parody
pattern
pen-pal letter
petition
photo essay
photograph
picture dictionary
plan (e.g., house, travel)
planet description
play
playing cards
poem
political cartoon
postage stamp
postcard
poster
prediction
press conference
prophecy
public service
  announcement
puppet show
puzzle

Q
quatrain
question
questionnaire
quilt
quiz

R
radio announcement
radio commercial
radio show
rap
rebus story
recipe
reply
report
reproduction
request
research report
résumé
review
rewrite
rhyme
riddle
role play
rubric

S
scenario
schedule
science fiction story
scrapbook
script
scroll
sculpture

seminar
series of letters
shopping list
short story
skit
sign
silk screen
simulation
slide show
slogan
soap opera
solution
solution to a community
  problem
song
speech
stencil
stick puppet
story
storyboard
story problem
subject dictionary
survey
symbol

T
tall tale
telegram
teach a class
theory (formulate and
  defend)
time line
tools
toy
training session

translation
transparency
travel advertisement
travel log
TV newscast

U
utopia (description)

V
Venn diagram
verdict
videotape
visual aid
vocabulary list

W
wall hanging
wanted poster
warmup
warrant for arrest
weather map
Web page
WebQuest
woodcut
word game
word search
word web
writing

Y
yearbook prediction

Z
zodiac chart
zoo map

6

Differentiated Assessment

Once again, in assessing students, we can't assume that one size fits all. The method of evaluation used should be a continuation of the type of differentiation used in the unit. In other words, assessment should be linked to the following:

- The method of performance during practice of a skill or concept

- Student learning styles

- Level of cognitive ability (Bloom's or another)

- Student skill level

In a differentiated classroom, there should also be separate grades given for three aspects:

- Growth (changes in performance, knowledge, or skills from the beginning to the end of the unit)

- Achievement (actual standards-based performance)

- Effort

Other than those basic concepts, there's actually nothing special or new about using assessment in a differentiated situation. Assessment, as always, should do the following:

- Be part of every day's activities: Students should be assessed before, during, and at the end of an instructional unit.

- Be formative: It should be a temperature check not just to measure knowledge but to give feedback to both teacher and student on how well students are doing, where there are gaps in learning, where students still have questions—and where students have exceeded expectations, too.

- Ask students to apply the knowledge and skills gained in basically the same way they have practiced that knowledge and those skills.

There should be a clear match between the expected outcomes of a unit and the tasks provided as the assessment.

♦ Be timely: Results should be quickly available to the student.

♦ Extend rather than merely measure knowledge.

♦ Never surprise students. Tell them what they'll learn, how to learn it, and how they'll know they've learned it. No pop quizzes, no surprise categories. Test what was taught, in the same manner in which it was practiced.

♦ Have clear criteria (a checklist or rubric) that communicate how students will be assessed.

Formal assessments often take the form of homework assignments, short performance tasks (such as a skit), dictations, and quizzes or tests over the entire contents of a unit. They, too, may be standardized, book generated, or homemade alternative, or performance, assessments, written or spoken or both, open-book, oral, or take-home, given to individuals or partners or groups.

Informal assessments show even more variety. Methods like Graffiti (a form of memory recall on paper listing words or concepts, facts or drawings in random order, as a quick snapshot of learning), Ticket Out, filling out graphic organizers or mind webs, journal entries, and just your own observations are good examples. Other possibilities include the following:

♦ Self-evaluation

♦ KWL (Know, Want to know, Learned)

♦ Peer evaluation

♦ Video

♦ Spot checks for progress

♦ Portfolio

♦ Drawing pictures

♦ Extended-time activities

♦ Deleting some options on a quiz or test

♦ Actual parts of a test taken separately over a longer period and assembled for a final grade (such as doing the speaking portion separately from the written)

Use Choice

Students who are evaluated primarily on one skill that they don't have (or think they don't) quickly get discouraged. I cannot stress enough the importance of using choice in assessments, as well as in teaching strategies, or in making sure that the assessments reflect the choices students have made in their learning strategies.

Show-What-You-Know Assessments

 This type of assessment is simply when students are allowed to demonstrate their knowledge or mastery of the required skills in a form they choose. For example, students might be allowed to do any five out of eight essay questions, or answer six out of 10 questions asked of them (writing or saying "pass" for the others). I might design a 55-point test and allow students to skip any five points (and because no section has only five points in it, they must still do something from every part of it).

I believe this approach mimics real life in any career. If I'm asked to help on a project at school, I can generally choose between leadership and helping roles, or I can choose whether to read, write, speak, or just provide refreshments (kinetic activity!). Allowing students to use the chapter skills in the way they are most comfortable with makes sense to me.

Providing open-ended questions is another form of choice, allowing students more leeway in their responses. For example, "Pick two famous people off the list provided, and describe them using two adjectives each"; "Choose three time periods in a typical school day, and for each, tell what you would usually be doing then"; "Plan a picnic for four friends, and tell what you'd buy and where." I like the words "choose" and "tell," because responses could be written or oral, live or on tape, and I often give my students a choice of those formats.

Another form of show what you know that I haven't tried yet involves a proposal written by the student. (For a project planner that would be easy to adapt to this, see the display on the next page.) The proposal should describe how the student intends to display their knowledge: a student-written short-answer or essay test, an oral or written report, a dramatic presentation, a mini-lesson, a three-dimensional or other creative project. (Warning: Make sure students don't suggest something they can get in its entirety from another source. Every such proposal must have enough of an in-class component that you know it is the student's own work.) This type of assessment does not have to take the place of a standardized test but rather would be an excellent study guide for the presenter and the class, perhaps earning bonus points on the test or having its grade averaged with the test.

Project Planner

Name(s): _____

Topic & Questions   **Due date:** _____

   Specific topic _____

   Specific questions to be answered: who/what/why/where/when:

_____

_____ (may go on attached sheet)

Resources (at least 3)   **Due date:** _____

   Print:_____

_____

   Internet:_____

_____

   Other:_____

Product Description   **Due date:** _____

   I/we'll be doing the following: _____

_____

Checklist   **Due date:** _____

You must complete the checklist for your type of project, and have a classmate fill out the checklist for you, too.

Sharing   **Due date:** _____

Here's how I plan to share my project with the class:

_____ display   _____ presentation

Evaluation Form   **Due date:**_____

Complete the Reflection form.

Bingo Exams

Teachers I've talked with at more than one school give a bingo-style final exam. In each box of the bingo grid is a category students need to speak or write about. Examples:

   ◆ Count from one to 20.

   ◆ Greet the teacher and ask how she is.

   ◆ List the month.

◆ Tell three things you like and two you don't.

If the students perform without errors, they get a stamp, and they may try a second time before it is crossed out as no longer valid. So, students choose which parts of the grid they'd like to try for a bingo (five in a row horizontally, vertically, or diagonally) for an A; four is a B, three is a C, and two is a D. They report that students appreciate having some control over a somewhat intimidating final exam and that students prepare carefully, because they only get two tries to pass. It takes longer to administer than a standard final exam, but in general the students get better grades and are more motivated.

Contracts

With a contract, students choose what they will do (the depth and quantity of work) for an agreed-upon grade. The contract is in writing, with clear penalties for late or unsatisfactory performance. Students who fail to compact out of a specific unit might design a contract for learning, with the teacher allowing them to work on enrichment activities during the portions of class instruction that the teacher agrees the student has mastered.

Students would definitely need assistance to stay on track and to complete the project on time. Checklists such as the ones at the end of this chapter help. A detailed step-by-step plan for completion, with one step to be completed each day, monitored by both the student and the teacher, are useful. I suggest using both.

Early finishers could, of course, do extra credit or have time to study or to do computer activities, but I'm afraid this would not appeal to many of my students who would expect this time to be free. Also, results could be plagiarized or just not good, because a large portion of the work for this would generally be done outside regular class time. I have not tried this method yet, because of my reservations about possible drawbacks:

Tiered Assessments

Because tiered lessons are trilevel (low, middle, high), it makes sense that the assessments for the end of a differentiated unit are equally stratified. After practicing the skills at varied levels (see Chapter 4 for a variety of tiered lessons), the final product or test should be adjusted to the manner in which students learned the skills. For most of the tiered lessons given as examples in Chapter 4, the easiest assessment would be to have students select one of their practice activities to do, without books or reference materials, as a grade for that unit.

If you are planning to give a standard book test, look at the test *before* you plan the tiered lessons, and make sure the practice activities for each level teach the skills in the manner in which they must be demonstrated on the test. If students need to write about a subject, all three tiered groups must do a written activity. If students must talk about it, they must do something oral.

If you plan to give each tier group a different form of performance assessment, pay careful attention to these considerations:

- Would students think each is comparable in terms of time and effort?

    Stronger students shouldn't be asked to do more work just because they can. And they will resent having to do something much more difficult for the same grade, and you'll hear from their parents as well. Think "separate but equal" when choices are offered.

- Do options allow for a variety of learning styles, interests, prior knowledge, and readiness?

    Don't despair at having to have several assessments; a variety of assessments is much less repetitive and boring to grade!

Use Context

As language teachers, we should all be using practice activities as well as assessments that put use of the language in context: Make students use the language as they would have to in a target-language situation or country. In such contexts, a multiple-choice test will just not do; instead, put students in a hypothetical situation and ask them to perform. Such an assessment is called an authentic or alternative or performance assessment, and there are entire books written on this topic, including mine. So here is a short summary:

Authentic assessments ask students to analyze, apply, and sometimes synthesize what they have learned. Even though students may not be able to choose their own topics or formats, there are usually multiple acceptable routes toward constructing an acceptable product or performance. And you as a teacher get a glimpse inside the student's head in viewing these constructed response answers.

Product Assessments

After a prompt or series of prompts, students produce a product that shows their understanding of and ability to use a concept or skill. This takes more time to complete than a select-a-response type. Examples include the following:

- Short-answer essay questions

- Show your work (For example, to show understanding of reasons for usage: underline imperfect tense verbs used for description, star those for ongoing action, box those for habitual actions)

- Concept maps

- Graphic representation (e.g., Venn diagram)

- Journal-type or letter-format response

- Stories or poems

- Research reports

- Extended journal responses

- Art exhibit

- Portfolio

- Newspaper

- Poster

See the ABCs list in Chapter 4, or the Gardner-oriented one at the end of this chapter.

Performance-Oriented Assessments (PBAs)

In this type, after a prompt or assignment or a series of prompts, students do something to show their understanding of the desired concepts and skills. Because performance-based assessments are complex, they are scored using rubrics that indicate levels of performance on a variety of parameters. Examples of Performance-Based Assessments (PBA) include the following:

- Performing a task such as purchasing something, checking into a hotel, ordering from a menu, describing a photograph

- Musical, dance, or dramatic performances (including exercise routines and fashion shows)

- Debate or discussion

- Athletic competition

- Oral presentation: report, skit, recitation, conversation

Following are some other good-to-use assessment strategies that involve placing things in context.

Personalized Assessment

Here I will just remind you of personalized assessments, previously discussed: students who chose their own vocabulary words to be tested on and wrote the quiz they would later take; students who proposed a project, outlined how they would accomplish it, and suggested criteria for its evaluation; and those on a WebQuest whose search led them in different directions and to different end results. All these students would have unique content and should be tested in a unique manner.

One more way to personalize, however, is a so-called focus-on-growth assessment. Using your classroom observations, students' scores on assignments, and comments made by the student on self-assessment questions and by partners in various groups, you can compile a sort of report card or an update, using a spreadsheet, a chart, or whatever method you find easiest, to give the student. If he or she knows that you notice effort as well as success and that classmates approve or disapprove of his or her behavior, it may make a difference.

Partner and Group Testing

Consider allowing students to choose whether they wish to be tested alone, with a partner, or in small groups. Each person should still receive an individual grade, but for some students, the thought of taking an exam (especially an oral one) one-on-one with a teacher is extremely frightening, and having a buddy along for moral support could result in a better performance. Remember once again, brain research tells us that when we're assessing, it is wise to re-create the learning situation. If this material was learned and practiced with a partner, or with the whole class interacting with the teacher, simply having a partner allows students to more closely simulate the learning situation, and the student has an easier time accessing what was learned. Especially if you have large classes, working with groups to test has other benefits: In terms of movement, it somehow seems easier to manage five groups of six than 30 individuals, and the group tests could be spread out over several class periods as well.

What does a group test look like? Usually, everyone in the group gets the same test paper. Note: These are not multiple-choice or true-or-false tests but, rather, ones in which students generate compositions, graphics, and sentences; respond to readings; and so on—and they're ones for which there may be more than one correct answer (e.g., masculine or feminine differences, differing opinions on a topic). Students in a group can work separately or talk to one another, but all write their own answers. Then you have two options: Let the group decide whose paper to turn in as their grade, or you can randomly choose one student (biggest shoe size, closest birthday, or whatever) to hand in his or her paper with the group's names on it.

If that is too nontraditional for you, here are some alternatives that you might consider:

◆ Give the test individually and then, during the last two minutes or so, let the students talk to anyone they want.

- Give students 30 seconds before the test to talk and write down anything they want, and allow them to use those notes during the test.

- Give a class grade: The whole class can talk to one another, and all need to write. Then collect the tests and put them in a pile. Correct only the first response on the first test paper, the second on the second paper, and so on. Everyone in the class gets the final grade, and the class will make sure the slackers work, because it affects their grade. I often do this when everyone did rather poorly on a test; I regive the same test or a similar one and then give an individual test on it later.

This method encourages the student-helping-student dynamic that brain research says is so good for long-term memory storage.

Use Variety

Don't always assess students in the same manner. Here are some strategies to add to your repertoire, if you don't already use them:

Knowledge Mapping

Knowledge mapping, a yearlong project, is a strategy used by many businesses, so teaching this to students might actually be teaching them a skill to use on a future job as well as in your classroom. To track the acquisition and loss of information and knowledge, knowledge mapping has three parts:

Survey   Audit   Synthesis

The user explores his or her own competencies and skills as well as those of others.

It is actually a sort of graphic, like a mind map, that students keep from the beginning of the year to the end and that will show them that they are adding to their knowledge. To make the map, students list what they know on the first day they begin, and then, as the class continues, they add grammar, vocabulary, and culture to it.

I know that every time my students master a new concept, I just push them to another new concept. This strategy helps them take stock of how far they have come since they began the class and is also available at semester exam time as a good listing of what might be on the test; it also shows them their own strengths and weaknesses.

These are some types of things to think of as you draw a knowledge map:

- What type of knowledge or skill is needed?
- Where can that knowledge be found?

- Who can help—that is, who do you go to when you have a problem?
- What would make your work easier?
- What happens when you are finished?

If you have computers available, right now on the Internet there is a free 30-day download to create a knowledge map and an example of how it works: http://www.thebrain.com/products/personalbrain/support/tutorials/pbtour.html.

Flex Fund

Think about setting aside a certain number of points for each grading period in a Flex Fund. My insurance company offers a Flex Fund–like discretionary funding program that allows me to tailor my insurance to meet my personal needs. In a classroom Flex Fund, students choose how they would like to earn their Flex Fund points, which usually are assigned to be the equivalent of one unit test grade. Options may include the following:

Class Participation

Give students a rubric that explains what good participation is. Here is a sample:

Criteria	Never	Sometimes	Always
Productive	0	3	4
Well timed	0	2	4
Prepared	0	2	4
Accurate	0	4	8

Other categories to consider adding to this rubric might be "listens well to others," "attendance," and "nondisruptive behavior" (sounds, gestures, and comments).

You also need to list (or have students help you list) activities that would apply: reading aloud, asking productive questions, offering answers, interpretations, or observations, participating in online blogs or key-pal experiences, after-school activities, and so on.

Close-Ups

A close-up is an in-depth investigation of a subject only touched on in class or in the book. It may involve an image or illustration, a list of facts or examples (e.g., of a grammar point and its exceptions), a news article, or other product.

Students would be expected to present their results to classmates in written or oral form or as a display, so everyone benefits from their research.

Leadership

Students could earn leadership points by leading a group, maintaining order and focus in the group or class, or tutoring another student.

Notebook Grades

Do you check and grade notebooks? Some teachers have students keep very precise notebooks, divided into sections such as vocabulary, rough drafts, grammar, class notes, and video work sheets. Then they give grades based on whether all student papers are in the notebook, organizational skills, neatness and completeness of work, whether mistakes have been corrected on all papers, whether notes have been rewritten and key information highlighted, and so on.

Other teachers actually give notebook quizzes with questions (described during the early weeks of the school year) about vocabulary words, about graded work, about daily or chapter objectives, about handouts, or about other activities done in class. If the notebook is properly maintained, students should be able to get 100 percent on the quiz.

Optional Test Grades

With this option, a student could choose to drop a low test score or double a high one. He or she could also take an optional review test or a test over a supplementary topic on which he or she has done some research or a report.

Special Projects

Such projects would be a written, an oral, or a visual report on supplementary readings (magazines, news articles, Internet sites) or films in the target language (TL), interviews (native speakers, people who use the TL on the job, other teachers who speak the TL or have visited a TL country), displays or models for the classroom, or other ideas students may propose. Be careful that these are not things they may simply "lift" from the Internet. These projects could be a good way for students to make connections with other subject areas: a book report on *Les Miserables* for both your class and English class, a report on a famous artist or a copy of a famous painting for art class, and so on.

Compacting

 With compacting—an assessment-based strategy thoroughly described in Chapter 4—students are pretested before beginning a new unit, and those who demonstrate mastery of a subject choose accelerated or other enrichment activities, such as supplemental reading, creative activities, or projects that they do while the other students learn the concept. At the end of a compacted unit, all students take the final assessment, even those who compacted out of the unit. Warning: There must be a reward to the more advanced students, either a higher grade or less homework, for example, or there will be no incentive to take advantage of compacting. Another term for the sort of independent study the advanced students do is an Orbital, in which they "spin off" to a topic of their own interest.

There is a compacting sheet in Chapter 4 (see page 73), or use the project planner and checklist that may be found on page 162.

Portfolios

Students have a natural tendency to save work (all those notebooks stuffed with crinkled papers and handouts!), and this strategy takes advantage of it. Portfolios are an effective way to get students to take a second look at their work and think about how they could improve. This is obviously a clear departure from the old "write, hand in, and forget" behavior, in which students consider a first draft to be a final product. A portfolio is a purposeful collection of student work that tells the story of a student's efforts, progress, or achievement in a given area over a period of time. A well-designed portfolio system can accomplish several important purposes: it can motivate students; it can provide explicit examples to parents, teachers, and others of what students know and are able to do; it allows students to chart their growth over time and to self-assess their progress; and it encourages students to engage in self-reflection.

Research shows that students at all levels see assessment as something that is done to them by someone else. Beyond percent correct, assigned letter grades, and grammatical or spelling errors, many students have little knowledge of what is involved in evaluating their work. Portfolios can provide structure and practice for students and involve them in developing and understanding criteria for good efforts, in coming to see the criteria as their own, and in applying the criteria to their own and other students' work.

When assigning a portfolio, consider these issues:

- ◆ **What will it look like?** There must be a physical description given (what documents are used and how they are stored) as well as a conceptual structure (work around a theme—e.g., best work, celebration, showcase, representative, or chronological order).

- ◆ **What goes in?** To make this decision, numerous other questions need to be addressed: What kinds of evidence will best show student progress toward learning goals? Will the portfolio contain best work only, a progressive record of student growth, or both? If you want to show growth, include student work from various times during the period. If best learning, have them choose what they consider to be their best effort.

♦ **How and when should items be selected?** Because student participation in the selection process is critical—so that students reflect on their work and monitor their own progress—materials that are included should be dated and include an explanation for their inclusion, called a reflection sheet. (Otherwise, over time, students may forget why they included a given item.) Working on assembling a portfolio is a good anchor activity (students can do it whenever they finish something else and have a spare moment in class). Early in the school year, have discussions with students to teach them to ask these questions:

- What would I like to reread or share with my parents or a friend?

- What makes a particular bit of class work a good product?

♦ **How and when should portfolios be evaluated?** Establish evaluation standards before the portfolio is begun. Portfolios are usually evaluated in terms of standards of excellence based on curriculum or in terms of growth demonstrated within an individual portfolio, rather than in terms of comparisons made among the portfolios of different students. Students' self-evaluation should explore areas needing more attention and effort as well as what they are now currently exploring and what their goals are for this class.

A portfolio is a process, not a destination. Good portfolios result from the following:

- ♦ Keeping the process simple

- ♦ Including more than just written work

- ♦ Asking students to explain and record why they chose each work sample

- ♦ Maintaining a clear purpose

- ♦ Ensuring that students have involvement and ownership

Projects

There are basically two ways to have students do projects: as a final unit assessment (or even a semester test) and by student choice.

As a believer in alternative methods of assessment, I have designed quite a few final projects for my students that demonstrate everything in the unit and have taken the place of a book-generated test.

For a unit on the imperfect versus the passé compos (Spanish: preterit), everyone in the class selects a different (famous) painting from a folder I've assembled (cut-apart old calendars). They are told that they were also there with those people, looking at the same scene. They must describe that day as a fond or scary or important memory: who was there, where they were, weather, clothing, who was doing what—and then suddenly (they must use the word Soudan) something new happened. They are to tell what happened immediately after the moment shown in the painting. I get some wonderful flights of fancy, and the students practice dictionary and diction skills as well as the two past tenses. They have choices of content, but not of product.

Another example is for the book *Le Petit Prince*. I have students create a new chapter, imitating the author's writing style and incorporating one or more of the characters and the general philosophy of the book, complete with an illustration and a quotable quote of their own making. This assessment tests everything we focus on during our readings. However, it may take the form of a PowerPoint presentation, a storyboard, a postcard, a standard chapter, a video, a rap, or a narrative poem. The students have choices of product, but not of content.

Finally, for level 1, our final project is a family book that we've been assembling since the first day of class. In each chapter we add another line for everyone in the family, so at the end of the semester, students review and finalize their writing and sit down with me and read me a portion of their book (or do it on tape) as an oral exam.

These are all examples of teacher-assigned projects that allow students to demonstrate competencies and knowledge.

The other type of project may be assigned not to an entire class but to select groups. You may remember that in compacting, students may select an activity to do while others do more traditional unit study. A project is one of their choices. Students who have a strong interest in a particular subject may wish to work with you or a community mentor to design an independent study of their interest area.

The most important element of any project is engage ability. To have a successful project, you need to arrange for each student:

- To be engrossed in learning something somewhat challenging
- To be involved in a real-world task or application
- To learn by doing
- To be able to effectively to diagnose where he or she is and what he or she should do next
- To communicate his or her learning

The second-most-important element is a good checklist or rubric so students are aware of what is required and are able to assess their own success while completing the project. See the section below for more on that topic.

Managing Grades

Keeping track of grades is always a concern, and you need to think about changes to make in your current policy. If you truly wish to differentiate, you will give grades for progress (growth), achievement (excellence), and effort (task completion).

Let's begin with the last one, the easiest: task completion. This means keeping track of all assignments and whether they have been done. Several creative teachers have a graphics approach to this type of assessment. Remember the tic-TAC-toe style vocab grid in Chapter 5 (page 104)? That could be used as an assessment: Take a stamp and for each activity they complete, award up to 20 points based on completion and accuracy (students will have used a checklist or rubric available to them on the wall or in a folder, so there should be no surprises), for a total of up to 100 points after the completion of five assignments. It is easy to see, at a glance, whether everything has been completed.

Another easy-to-use assignment is a homework calendar, an example of which is found on page 33. Students who are absent are still expected to have work in on the day it is due or on the day they return. Ms. Saragovia also uses a stamp, saying: "When students arrive, they are to place their homework calendar and homework on their desk and do their warmup. If the homework is not out, I do not stamp it. It's rough in September, but then it gets easier."

If students are doing projects, make sure you break them down into steps, such as these:

◆ Topic handed in and approved

◆ Detailed plan

◆ List of sources

◆ Rough draft

◆ Peer evaluation

Dedicate a spot in the grade book for each step. If the class is differentiating for product, it is quite likely that students will reach these steps at different times. A glance at the grade book (or a checklist on the wall) will tell both you and the students who is making progress and who needs to proceed faster.

The second easiest is excellence: This would be the final grade for the project, or the chapter- or unit-assessment score.

The grade you'll probably need to think about is the one for growth. This should take two forms:

- Self-assessment by the student

- Assessment by the teacher

Both forms of assessment should use the same rubric, one that is given to students the first week of classes.

Rubrics

A rubric is a list of explicit criteria for assessing student performance or product.

There are basically two types of rubric: holistic and analytical. A holistic rubric (see display below) evaluates the performance overall and rates it in a qualitative manner.

Holistic Rubric for Growth

Unsatisfactory: Student demonstrates little growth. Makes little or no effort. Work consistently missing, late, or partial. Does not participate voluntarily. Problems with behavior.

Standard barely met: Student is beginning to learn a few skills. Work closely resembles that of other students, with little originality. Work done on time. Participates occasionally.

Meets standard: Student work demonstrates consistent growth over time. Student is beginning to assume decision-making roles. Work shows more than minimal effort to complete. Participates often in class.

Exceeds standard: Student demonstrates ownership, passion, and commitment to the subject. Works consistently on his or her own to analyze, synthesize, organize, or apply knowledge in novel situations, resulting in unique responses. Leads and assists classmates in studies.

The next display (page 175) is an example of a holistic rubric for student and teachers to use to assess behavior.

Holistic Rubric for Behavior

Daily Performance Grade		Criteria
9–10	Exceeds the standard	Helps facilitate classroom activity Demonstrates engaged, active learning throughout the period Makes consistently strong contributions to the classroom
8	Meets the standard	Participates in a generally constructive way Demonstrates engaged, active learning through part of the class period Makes some strong contributions to the classroom
7	Approaches the standard	Has little negative or positive effect on the class May be grappling with concepts but shows little evidence of learning Prepares, but makes little contribution to the classroom
5–6	Falls below the standard	Has more of a negative effect on the class than positive Required work or preparation incomplete Disruptive behavior makes learning difficult for others Has trouble staying on task; needs to be reminded
0	Fails to meet standard	Sent out of class or truant Refuses to stay on task Sleeps

An analytical rubric breaks the performance down into the different levels of behavior expected, assigning each a point value (which can be weighted if desired); points are totaled for a quantitative measure. An example of an analytical rubric for growth may be seen in the display on the following page.

Analytical Rubric

	1 *Standard not met*	2 *Standard barely met*	3 *Meets standard*	4 *Exceeds standard*
Work/ effort	Work is not done or is done late Plagiarism or copying Sleeping, tardiness or excessive absence	Grammatically incorrect, simple sentences, misspellings common Work is done on time	Work mostly correct Works well on own or in group	Work done well (more than minimum effort) Shows leadership
Skill	Uses English frequently No attempt to use new vocabulary or structures	Uses a few English words Little attempt to use new vocabulary or structures	Consistently attempts to use target language	Succeeds in using new vocabulary No English used
Behavior Attitude	Comments incomprehensible, inappropriate, or disruptive	Obeys all rules with occasional reminder needed	Enthusiastic and cooperative	Encourages and helps others Exceeds expectations

The purpose the weekly composition is to improve overall writing skills and to practice current vocabulary and grammar; a rubric is shown below.

Rubric for a Weekly Composition

	1	2	3	4
Content	Does not address prompt	Addresses part of prompt	General comments only	Responds to all parts of prompt
Vocabulary	Uses only basic vocabulary	Has several poor word choices Has awkward phrasing	Uses several new vocabulary words	Uses many words from recent study
Grammar	Makes little attempt to use focus grammar	Makes many errors in focus grammar usage	Makes some errors in focus grammar usage	Grammar usage is perfect or nearly perfect

Organization	Is difficult or impossible to follow	Attempt apparent	Is mostly logical	Is logical and thoughtful
Mechanics and spelling	Fails to proofread	Has several important errors	Has one or two major errors	Is perfect or nearly perfect
			Total: _____	/20 points

You can find a great resource for writing analytical rubrics of many types at http://www.teach-nology.com/web_tools/rubrics.

Checklists

Another type of rubric, a checklist is exactly what it sounds like: a list of behaviors to look for; the student records the presence or absence of that attribute by checking or circling that action. Following are several types of checklists that may be used by students as they do projects described in chapters 4, 5, or 6 of this book.

Checklist: *Poster*
(Note: The below description is for an "A" poster!)

Names (Student) _____ (Classmate) _____

Student   **Classmate**

Student	Classmate	
_____	_____	Color is used.
_____	_____	Picture or illustration is large.
_____	_____	All writing large enough to read from across the room.
_____	_____	Neat (not messy).
_____	_____	Organized.
_____	_____	All important information found on poster.
_____	_____	Accurate information.
_____	_____	Correct spelling.
_____	_____	Correct grammar.
_____	_____	Creativity of presentation.
_____	_____	Interesting to look at and read.
_____	_____	Student's name is on project.

Checklist: ***PowerPoint Presentation***

Names (Student) _____ (Classmate) _____

Student   **Classmate**

Student	Classmate	
____	____	Information up-to-date.
____	____	Information interesting.
____	____	Picture appropriate.
____	____	Sound appropriate (sound is optional).
____	____	Effects (optional) used: enhance, distract.
____	____	Pacing not too slow, not too fast.
____	____	Well organized.
____	____	Font color contrasts sharply from background.
____	____	Font size easy to read across room.
____	____	Font style easy to read.
____	____	Correct spelling.
____	____	Correct grammar.
____	____	Student's name is on project.

Checklist: ***Video***

Names (Student) _____ (Classmate) _____

Student   **Classmate**

Student	Classmate	
____	____	Sound quality good.
____	____	Dress and props appropriate.
____	____	Pace: not too slow, not too fast.
____	____	Seriousness of performers.
____	____	Accurate information.
____	____	Correct pronunciation.
____	____	Correct grammar.
____	____	Interesting beginning.
____	____	Interesting ending.

Checklist: ***Brochure***

Names (Student) _____ (Classmate) _____

Student   **Classmate**

Student	Classmate	
____	____	Illustrations mixed with text where appropriate.
____	____	Well organized (no repetitions).
____	____	Information up-to-date.
____	____	Information correct.
____	____	Well-balanced layout on page.
____	____	Correct spelling.

Student	Classmate	
____	____	Correct grammar.
____	____	Student's name is on project.

Checklist: *Mobile*

Names (Student) _____ (Classmate) _____

Student	Classmate	
____	____	Colorful.
____	____	Easy to read.
____	____	Easy to understand why elements were chosen.
____	____	Accurate information.
____	____	Correct spelling.
____	____	Correct grammar.
____	____	Student's name is on project.

Checklist: *Storyboard*

Names (Student) _____ (Classmate) _____

Student	Classmate	
____	____	Setting is clear.
____	____	Characters have names and personalities.
____	____	Conflict (man vs. man, nature, self) exists.
____	____	Several actions take place.
____	____	Uses several words of vocab from the unit.
____	____	Uses several elements from the original story.
____	____	Uses color.
____	____	Writing neat and legible.
____	____	Correct spelling.
____	____	Correct grammar.

Checklist: *Oral (10 points)*

Names (Student) _____ (Classmate) _____

Student	Classmate	
____	____	Understood question or prompt.
____	____	Spoke more than basic requirements (offered supporting examples and details).
____	____	Spoke with ease or flow and enthusiasm.
____	____	Used a variety of sentence structure and vocabulary.
____	____	Spoke at an appropriate volume level.
____	____	Evidence of preparation.
____	____	Made eye contact.

____	____	Correct pronunciation.
____	____	Correct grammar.
____	____	Spoke for an appropriate length of time.

Checklist: ***Listening Activity***
                (three points for each question or response)
            Responses may be written or oral (no matching!)
Student's Name _____

____ Didn't require more than one repetition.
____ Complete response.
____ No errors in response.

Note: Another item I sometimes put in: one point for a basic response, and two points for an elaborated response. Example: If the prompt is "What sports do you play?" an elaborated response would be not just the sport, but where, when, and with whom they play it, or that they won a game.

Checklist: ***Written (20 points)***
Names (Student) _____ (Classmate) _____

Student	**Classmate**	
____	____	On task in class.
____	____	Objectives met.
____	____	Correct format for paper (font, etc.).
____	____	Neatness.
____	____	Ideas clearly expressed.
____	____	Easily understood by intended audience.
____	____	Careful choice of words.
____	____	Content shows knowledge of subject.
____	____	Specific details are used related to topic.
____	____	Details are accurate.
____	____	Organized presentation.
____	____	Variety of sentence structures.
____	____	Variety of vocabulary used.
____	____	Illustrations (if appropriate).
____	____	Characterization good (if appropriate).
____	____	Evidence of editing.
____	____	Title reflects subject.
____	____	Correct spelling.
____	____	Correct grammar.
____	____	Student's name is on project.

Checklist: ***Flip book***

_____   _____   Required size.
_____   _____   Five different categories.
_____   _____   At least two details for each category.
_____   _____   Easy to use.
_____   _____   Correct spelling.
_____   _____   Correct grammar.
_____   _____   Student's name is on project.

Checklist: ***T-Shirt***

_____   _____   Uses color.
_____   _____   Uses information from research or reading.
_____   _____   Meaning easily understood.
_____   _____   Appropriate for school wear.
_____   _____   Correct spelling.
_____   _____   Correct grammar.
_____   _____   Oral presentation of product to class.

Checklist: ***Storybook***

_____   _____   Setting clear.
_____   _____   Characters have names and personalities.
_____   _____   Conflict (man vs. man, nature, self) exists.
_____   _____   Several actions take place.
_____   _____   Uses several words of vocab from the unit.
_____   _____   Has obvious moral, meaning, or theme.
_____   _____   Uses color.
_____   _____   Writing neat and legible.
_____   _____   Correct spelling.
_____   _____   Correct grammar.

The student uses the appropriate checklist while completing the project, and then he or she has the project checked by a classmate before handing it in. I like to have projects peer-checked for several reasons:

- ◆ Students need to have projects done a bit in advance of deadline in order to have time for someone else look it over.

- ◆ Students might hand in something junky if it were for my eyes only, but they take more care if a classmate will see it.

- ◆ There is always a chance that the classmate, when reading another project, will see in it things that he or she could improve in his or her own project.

- ◆ The fewer errors in a product, the faster the grading process goes for me!

A Few Final Thoughts

Here are a few more things to remember about assessment:

- ◆ An assessment is not a test at the end of a unit. It is ongoing.
- ◆ Students need multiple ways to demonstrate their learning.
- ◆ Assessments identify both what is right and what is wrong, and suggest how to fix what is wrong.

Assessments Classified by Gardner's Intelligences

Verbal/ Linguistic Say it Write it	Advertisement Anecdote Book report Brochure Bulletin board Commercial Comparison Creative writing Crossword Debate Description Dialogue Diary	Discussion Drama Essay Explanation Interview Journal Lesson Letter Menu Monologue News article Newscast Oral report Outline	Panel discussion Parody Plan Play Poem Poster Prediction Radio broadcast Recipe Recitation Report Riddle	Role play Script Simulation Socratic seminar Song Speech Telephone message Weather forecast Word search
Visual/Spatial Picture it	Album cover Art project Award Banner Bookmark Book jacket Bulletin board Cartoon	Clothing Diorama Flag Flip book Flowchart Game Graph Hat	Illustration Ketch Mask Map Model Movie Mural Painting	Portrait Postage stamp Poster Rebus story Scroll Sculpture Storyboard T-shirt Video
Logical/ Mathematical Count it	Bibliography Brainteaser Bulleted list Chart	Checklist Comparison Flowchart Game	Graph Map Menu Maze	Outline Puzzle Riddle Time line Travel log

Bodily/ Kinesthetic Move it	Art project Ballet or other dance Card game Clothing Demonstration	Diorama Display Dramatization Flip book Food Gadget	Game Instrument Learning center Machine or invention	Mime Model Puppets Puzzle Video
Musical/ Rhythmic Hum it	Album Audio Ballad/rap/ song	Choral reading Concert Dance	Jingle recording Lyrics	Poem/rhyme Song Video
Interpersonal Lead it	Advice Discussion	Interview Mentor	Plan an event	Survey class opinions and present results
Intrapersonal Reflect on it	Advice	Book report	Journal	Self-evaluation
Naturalistic Investigate it	Bulletin board Collection	Description Guess	Observation Photo essay	Scrapbook

7

Reflections on Differentiation

Here, in a nutshell, is why I decided to try differentiation in my classroom. Modern brain research has confirmed what experienced teachers have always known:

- ♦ No two children are alike.

- ♦ No two children learn in identical ways.

- ♦ An enriched environment for one student is not necessarily enriched for another.

- ♦ In the classroom we should teach children to think for themselves.

Obviously, the curriculum and learning goals will be the same for all students, but the methodology used should be varied to make a better fit for each student. That's what differentiation is all about.

But it's a bit scary, going outside one's comfort zone and trying new things. Differentiation involves six basic challenges for teachers:

- ♦ To alter classroom management style

- ♦ To modify recording practices

- ♦ To provide a wider range of resources

- ♦ To reorganize the classroom

- ♦ To introduce (slowly) alternative teaching practices, such as flexible grouping, independent study, and preassessments (and more)

- ♦ To extend and modify the timetable

Teachers are as different as their students. Some will naturally differentiate; others are a bit frightened by the prospect. Remember to balance your own needs with those of the students. Once again, there are no recipes. The following guidelines will help you begin to differentiate or refine your differentiation:

- Make sure you have a plan for managing differentiation: giving directions, meaningful student motion, and making sure students know what is expected of them (e.g., where to put finished work).

- Frequently reflect on how well what you want to do matches your results. If there's a mismatch, talk to colleagues about what you could do differently.

- Start with a mental image of what you want to accomplish, and then plan.

- Remember to talk with students frequently about what you are doing with them, why you are doing it, how well it is working, and what they can do to help.

- Try to view differentiation as a cumulative process. Begin slowly, just one new thing at a time. Choose just one unit or one element (content, process, product, or learning environment). Work at a pace you can handle.

- Arrange to evaluate in a way so that you can notice change: Did it go well?

- Monitor frequently, discuss results, and fine-tune with student input.

- Take time off to recharge: Differentiation is just one of the tools in your arsenal of strategies.

- Try to enjoy yourself. Recognition that I can still learn new things is one of my greatest joys in teaching, and the knowledge that your students can help you learn new words and methods is empowering for them as well. Mine love to bring me songs, articles, and information gleaned from magazines and television on topics learned in class. A student brought in the classic song "Aux Champs-Elysées" in a much more updated version by NOFX (a rock group), something I can now share with all my students.

One of the first facts I have had to face is that I cannot possibly provide daily assignments that match the range of levels of all the students in my class, individually. It is not always possible, for example, to find or create leveled reading resources on topics such as the Louvre's treasures or the Tour de France. So, most of the week, I assign my students the same material in the text or workbook. Once or twice weekly, however, I do provide a choice of assignments. I can see that in time, I will be able to offer my students more and more choices.

Small classes are the ideal place to differentiate. It is a lot harder with a bigger class, which takes a *lot* of organizing.

It is another major concept of differentiation—flexible grouping—that I really have had to wrestle with. Arranging my classes into adjustable groups for skill work or assignments has proven difficult at best. The reasons for this are as follows:

♦ Some tasks or assignments call for groups based on interest.

♦ Some call for groups based on learning style.

♦ Some call for groups based on student readiness; whether or not they have the skills—reading, writing, analysis, organization—required to complete the work.

Deciding who goes in which group takes quite a bit of time, thought, and organization.

Graphics

I am a visual learner, and graphics help me. Here are two more visuals that have helped guide me in differentiating.

The display that follows is a representation of a short lesson to teach a skill such as reflexive verbs, before and after differentiation.

One Lesson: Before and After Differentiation

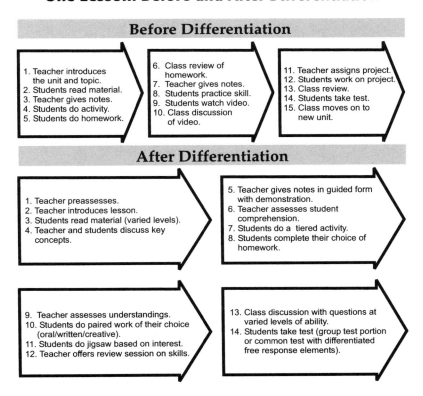

The next display graphically illustrates, in tic-tac-toe format, the elements of differentiation, and how they are related.

The Relationship of Differentiation Elements

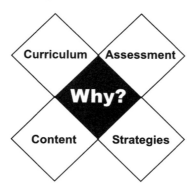

Go counterclockwise from the bottom left corner.

The "Content" box asks: What do my students need to know? What is the best way to deliver that information?

"Strategies" is where you decide what strategies will be best for students, based on learning styles and preferences, brain research, time constraints, and perhaps student input.

At the top right corner is "Assessment": What product or performance will be required? What will students need to complete the performance or product? Consider formative and summative feedback as well as self-evaluation.

"Curriculum" and essential learnings asks: What lifelong skills will students need in real life, to benefit their community and family?

And between them all is the big question "Why?": Why do this? This is where you should return to take a look at the standards and curriculum, the state and local benchmarks for the level. Make sure whatever you have planned relates to those.

Now use it to play tic-tac-toe. For example, let's say you have determined the information and required skills for the unit; so place an X there. Then ask why, and check the standards to see exactly what they are and place an X there. Then move to the upper right: if the product doesn't practice those skills, there would be an O, and no one wins. Likewise, if the assessment is good and aligned with the standard, but the content isn't aligned with both, we also haven't designed a quality learning experience.

You should try to connect your plans horizontally as well as vertically, always passing through the center square. If everything is aligned, all will go well.

Frequently Asked Questions

I like the way I teach. If it's working, why change it?

Trying out new strategies is hard work at first, and you may feel less secure. But if we're honest, we all have students who struggle and just don't succeed, and we wish and wonder how we could do a better job. These students *will* benefit from differentiation.

With the focus not on what we teach but on what and how students learn, we increase the likelihood that all students will be at least partially successful. And here's a really good benefit: Students who are succeeding are motivated to do the tasks presented to them, which means far fewer behavior-management problems. Remember, too, that most things that are really rewarding are complicated.

Also, students aren't the only ones who benefit from differentiation. Just as they benefit from variety, so will you. Differentiation requires a different kind of energy than does direct instruction. It's more engaging for the teacher.

What do you like most about differentiated activities?

I teach on a block schedule. This is ideal for differentiated activities, which might take a couple of weeks to complete on a regular schedule, with shorter periods. On the block, differentiation generates a workshop-style environment, which may look a bit chaotic to an outsider (though my administrators like what they see happening, as well as the results we get). I just move around my classroom, acting as facilitator with each group.

On a schedule, such as the alternating block, on which you wouldn't see students every day, the differentiation method is ideal, because students are expected to continue work on their project even on the off day. This means that the students definitely understand what work they need to do as well as how to do it, preventing an often-reported problem by A/B block teachers who don't differentiate. The use of grids, checklists, and scaffolding such as those found in earlier chapters makes it easy for students to continue work outside a classroom (and makes it very hard for them to claim they got stuck or didn't know what to do).

I don't choose the content and skills I teach; that's in the local, district, and state curriculum. And in light of the fact that the students need to pass their assessment, how can I take the time to differentiate?

Differentiated classes are the *best* response to standards-based education. In a differentiated classroom, no student is left behind, and advanced students don't have to wait for the slower ones before they can move on. Curriculum is just the destination and doesn't dictate how you reach that destination.

How do I find the time in class to differentiate?

You may actually *save* time, because differentiated instruction lets you use your time more efficiently. You won't waste time teaching content to students who've already mastered it (remember compacting?), and you'll be available for the students who need your attention.

How can I find the planning time to differentiate?

It's true that the bulk of the work is in the up-front planning. Differentiation *does* require additional time. The key is to do the following:

+ Start small. Just take a good look at one unit and differentiate that. And every unit you differentiate this year will be there next year for you to use again.

+ Form partnerships or groups of those interested in trying differentiation. Do a book study together, or try action research. Don't forget your colleagues, at the local or the Internet level. (I find FLTEACH, an e-mail list for language teachers, to be a valuable resource for this.) If there are even two teachers in your subject area, and each one of you differentiates a unit and you share, then you have two units. AATF offers mentors for "single" teachers; so do AATSP and the other AAT groups.

When teachers take on problem solving as a group, the group's support (and struggles—you won't be the only one with the occasional bad lesson!) will help a lot. What also will help—and make you more likely to carry through on your ideas and not give up—is the idea that other people expect you to try these things and are hoping for your success.

And don't stop with just colleagues. When you've had a measure of success, go on to the next level: Share what you're doing with administrators and parents. Ask them to observe and help as well. You might be surprised at the results.

How do I make changes in how I teach when there's no budget for training, materials, or resources?

Differentiation doesn't require new books or supplies. It's a collection of strategies, procedures, and behaviors. But if your administrator genuinely supports professional development, perhaps he or she can get a substitute to free you up for planning or to meet with other teachers in a department or grade level to swap units and ideas.

I'm uncomfortable with the idea of challenging all students. Won't it be hard to make students and parents believe that giving the same grade for different levels of work is fair?

First, let's talk about challenge. Challenge doesn't mean *more* work, just work of a different kind. Use Bloom's levels of thinking to select an activity at a higher level. Of course, students will resent being asked to take on a challenge if it's more work. The key is to give less work, but more challenging work.

Second, don't forget to let students select their own level of participation. We all know students who aren't good at spelling, memorizing, and remembering facts, who can easily do a synthesis activity. Every student needs the opportunity to work at all levels. So, if you let the student select, instead of assigning him or her to a level, there should be no problem with the perception of fairness from that student or the parents.

Third, don't worry that students who select the upper levels will miss out on the basics. By the very nature of Bloom's, the higher levels reteach and reinforce the basics below them. For example, if you ask students to critique the ending of a story, they must know the basic vocabulary, facts, concepts, and writing methods used in the story.

Finally, the most critical variable in all this is your *will to succeed*. If you think you can, then you can. If you think you can't, you won't.

A final image (from Tomlinson, 2001): The classroom as an escalator going higher with each effort.

Bibliography

Articles

Armstrong, T. (1989). Little geniuses [Electronic version]. *Parenting*, September. Retrieved February 5, 2006, from http://www.thomasarmstrong.com/articles/geniuses.htm

Claxton, C. S. (1990). Learning styles, minority students, and effective education. *Journal of Developmental Education, 14*, 6–8, 35.

Jacobs, H., & Borland, J. (1986). The interdisciplinary concept model: Theory and practice. *Gifted Child Quarterly, 30*(4), 159–163.

Sternberg, R. J., Torff, B., & Grigorenko, E. L. (1998). Teaching triarchically improves student achievement. *Journal of Educational Psychology, 90*(3), 374–384.

Taylor, C. W. (1974). Multiple talent teaching. *Today's Education.* 71–74.

Tomlinson, C. (2002). Invitations to learn. *Educational Leadership, 1*, 6–10, 60.

Books

Benjamin, A. (2002). *Differentiated instruction: A guide for middle and high school teachers.* Larchmont, NY: Eye On Education.

Benjamin, A. (2003). *Differentiated instruction: A guide for elementary school teachers.* Larchmont, NY: Eye On Education.

Bloom, B., Englehart, M., Furst, E., Hill, W., & Krathwohl, D. (1956). *Taxonomy of educational objectives: The classification of educational goals. Handbook I: Cognitive domain.* New York: Longmans, Green.

Buzan, Tony (1989). *Use your head.* London: BBC Consumer Publishing.

Buzan, Tony (2002). *How to Mind Map.* New York: HarperCollins.

Csikszentmihalyi, M. (1997). *Finding flow: The psychology of engagement with everyday life.* New York: BasicBooks.

Danielson, C. (1996). *Enhancing professional practice: A framework for teaching.* Alexandria, VA: Association for Supervision and Curriculum Development (ASCD).

Etzioni, A. (1993). *The spirit of community: Rights, responsibility, and the communitarian agenda.* New York: Crown.

193

Fisher, C. W., Berliner, D. C., Filby, N. N., Marliave, R., Cahen, L. S., & Dishaw, M. M. (1980). Teaching behaviors, academic learning time, and student achievement: An overview. In C. Denham & A. Lieberman (Eds.), *Time to learn*. Washington, DC: National Institute of Education.

Gardner, H. (1991). *The unschooled mind: How children think and how schools should teach*. New York: BasicBooks.

Heacox, D. (2002). *Differentiating instruction in the regular classroom: How to reach and teach all learners, grades 3–12*. Minneapolis, MN. Free Spirit.

Hirsch, E. D., Jr. (1987). *Cultural literacy: What every American needs to know*. Boston: Houghton Mifflin.

Hunter, Madeline. (1994). *Mastery Teaching: Increasing instructional effectiveness in elementary and secondary schools, colleges, and universities*. Thousand Oaks, CA: Corwin Press.

Jensen, E. (1998). *Teaching with the brain in mind*. Alexandria, VA: Association for Supervision and Curriculum Development.

Joyce, B. R., Weil, M., & Calhoun, E. (2003). *Models of teaching* (6th ed.). Boston: Allyn & Bacon.

Marsden, Chantal (1994). *Harrap's French Exercises*. New York: Macmillan.

Marzano, Robert J., and Pickering, Debra J. (1997). *Dimensions of learning teacher's manual*, 2nd edition. Alexandria, VA: Association for Supervision and Curriculum Development.

McCarthy, Bernice, & McCarthy, Dennis. (2005). *Teaching around the 4MAT Cycle*. Thousand Oaks, CA: Corwin Press.

Reis, S. M., & Renzulli, J. S. (1997) *The schoolwide enrichment model: A how-to guide for educational excellence* (2nd ed.). Creative Learning Press.

Renzulli, Joseph S. (2003). *Enrichment clusters: A practical plan for real-world, student-driven learning*. Mansfield Center, CT: Creative Learning Press, Inc.

Sousa, D. A. (1995). *How the brain learns*. Reston, VA: National Association of Secondary School Principals.

Tomlinson, C. A. (1999). *The differentiated classroom: Responding to the needs of all learners*. Alexandria, VA: Association for Supervision and Curriculum Development (ASCD).

Tomlinson, Carol. (2001). *How to differentiate instruction in mixed-ability classrooms*. Alexandria, VA: Association for Supervision and Curriculum Development (ASCD).

Tomlinson, Carol. (2002). Invitations to Learn. *Educational Leadership, 1*, 6–10, 60.

Vygotsky, L. (1986). *Thought and language*. Cambridge, MA: MIT Press.

Websites

Accuweather. Retrieved 3 February 2006 from http://www.accuweather.com

The Amazing Flash Card Machine. Retrieved 5 February 2006 from http://www.flashcardmachine.com/

Blogger. Retrieved 5 February 2006 from http://www.blogger.com/start

Filamentality. Retrieved 5 February 2006 from BlueWeb'n site: http://www.bluewebn.com/wired/fil/index.html

FLTEACH: Foreign Language Teaching Forum. Retrieved 5 February 2006 from http://www.cortland.edu/flteach/

Inspiration: Free trial. Retrieved 4 February 2006 from http://www.inspiration.com/general_biz.html

Jester, Catherine. *A Learning style survey for college.* Retrieved 28 January 2006 from http://www.metamath.com/multiple/multiple_choice_questions.html

Learning Styles Survey. Retrieved 28 January 2006 from http://www3.interscience.wiley.com:8100/legacy/college/strahler/0471417416/lss/survey.html

McKenzie, Walter (1999) *Multiple Intelligences Inventory.* Retrieved 28 January 2006 from http://www.surfaquarium.com/MI/inventory.htm

Organization practice: Mapping. Retrieved 5 February 2006 from http://www.coun.uvic.ca/learn/program/hndouts/class1.html

Organization practice: Concept Map Retrieved 5 February 2006 from http://www.coun.uvic.ca/learn/program/hndouts/class1a.html

Personal Brain. Demonstration and download. Retrieved 5 February 2006 from http://www.thebrain.com/products/personalbrain/support/tutorials/pbtour.html

Quia Web. Online quizzes. Retrieved 31 January 2006from http://www.quia.com

Quizlab. Retrieved 31 January 2006 from http://www.funbrain.com

Teachnology: Web Tools for Educators. Rubrics, Rubric makers. Retrieved 5 February 2006 from http://www.teach-nology.com/web_tools/rubrics/

TrackStar. WebQuest writing site. Retrieved 5 February 2006 from http://trackstar.4teachers.org.

Weather Underground. Retrieved 4 February 2006 from http://www.wunderground.com

What's Your Learning Style. Retrieved 28 January 2006 from http://www.ldpride.net/learning_style.html